NEXT YEAR IN JERUSALEM

PHOTOGRAPHS BY MAX-MOSHE & HILLA JACOBY

Introduction by Teddy Kollek

Text by Tim Dowley & Heike Goshen

The Golden Gate, Jerusalem.

NEXT YEAR IN JERUSALEM

PHOTOGRAPHS BY MAX-MOSHE & HILLA JACOBY

Introduction by Teddy Kollek

Text by Tim Dowley & Heike Goshen

HARVEST
HOUSE
PUBLISHERS

Eugene, Oregon 97402

Scripture quotations in this book are taken from the King James Version of the Bible.

Endpapers: Detail of the mosaic floor of the fifth-century A.D. church at Madaba, Transjordan, showing a detailed map of Byzantine Jerusalem. The columns of the *Cardo Maximus* can clearly be seen.

NEXT YEAR IN JERUSALEM

Copyright © 1995 Hänssler Verlag KG, Neuhausen, Germany Design © 1995 Three's Company Angus Hudson Ltd.

First published in North America by Harvest House Publishers, 1075 Arrowsmith, Eugene, Oregon 97402-9197, USA

ISBN 1-56507-3428

Designed and created by Three's Company 12 Flitcroft Street, London WC2H 8DJ

Enquiries from publishers to: Angus Hudson Ltd., Concorde House, Grenville Place, London NW7 3SA, United Kingdom Tel + 44 181 959 3668 Fax + 44 181 959 3678

Printed in Singapore.
95 96 97 98 99 00 01 – 10 9 8 7 6 5 4 3 2 1

Acknowledgments
All photographs by Hilla and Max-Moshe Jacoby except the following:

Zev Radovan: endpapers, p.76
Tiger Colour Library: pp. 11 (top), 19 (top), 27, 31, 40, 72, 73, 74 (bottom), 75, 78 (bottom left), 88 (top), 89, 90 (both), 95, 100, 114-115, 120-121, 130 (left), 131 (bottom), 134 (top), 135 (bottom), 149 (top left), 168 (both), 169 (top), p.231
Ancient Art and Architecture Collection: pp. 9, 10-11, 12 (bottom), 13 (bottom), 18
Dieter Schäfer: pp. 8, 12-13 (top), 28-29, 32-33 (bottom), 37, 41, 48, 50-51, 55, 58-59, 74 (top), 76-77, 90 (bottom), 150-151, 154-155, 156-157, 159, 201

NEXT YEAR IN JERUSALEM

CONTENTS

1.
Introduction p. 7

2.
The Story of Jerusalem p. 25

3.
The Old City—and Beyond p. 61

4.
The Western Wall p. 111

5.
A Hundred Gates p. 137

6.
Jesus and Jerusalem p. 147

7.
City of Gold, Copper, and Light p. 171

8.
Jerusalem—a Modern City p. 195

9.
An Everlasting Memorial p. 213

10.
Feasts and Festivals p. 223

Index
p. 253

The photographers

Max-Moshe and Hilla Jacoby form an internationally renowned photographic team. They have held their own photographic exhibitions in many different countries.

Between 1978 and 1994 Max-Moshe and Hilla Jacoby created fourteen photographic books, including *The Land of Israel, Hallelujah Jerusalem, New York–New York, Sweden, The Jews, God's People, Israel the Miracle,* and many others.

Max-Moshe is the recipient of four gold medals, together with the cultural award of his birthplace, Coblenz, Germany. Twice honored with the Kodak book award, for some years Max-Moshe and Hilla have undertaken sound-and-vision lecture tours featuring their presentation: *His Land–His People.*

1

Introduction

**"The LORD doth build up Jerusalem:
he gathereth together the outcasts of Israel."**
(Psalm 147:2)

The Damascus Gate into the Old City.

Opposite: A medieval world map dating from 1275 which shows Jerusalem at the center of the world.

Introduction

Jerusalem—most people feel something special when they hear the name of this city, Holy City to the world's three major monotheistic religions. Jerusalem's trimillennium as the Jewish capital will be celebrated in 1996 by millions of people—in the city itself, around Israel, and all over the world.

It is not an easy task to describe what it is exactly that makes this city so extraordinarily fascinating and intriguing. It is a most beautiful, wonderful city, and readers will have to forgive my enthusiasm, since I have been in love with it for almost thirty years!

Jerusalem has many faces. The Bible praises it with more than a hundred names. Jerusalem's physical beauty alone provides a unique atmosphere. Being situated 800 meters (2600 feet) above sea level, and being for Jews their spiritual, religious, and political capital,

Hebrew speakers "ascend to Jerusalem" literally and emotionally.

Depending upon which of its seven hills visitors find themselves on, the city offers a different view. Towards the west, one can discern the green fields and orchards of the coastal plain, imagining the skyline of Tel Aviv and the mist above the Mediterranean coast some 60 kilometers (45 miles) away. In the south and east, the Judean desert spreads its magnificently colored hills, and if the weather is clear—which it is most of the time—one can discern the distant bluish outline of the Dead Sea, 403 meters (1300 feet) below sea level. Far below the city flows the Jordan River, and beyond it stretch the Moabite mountains, with their breathtaking panorama.

Every bit as varied and contrasting as the views surrounding Jerusalem are the sights within the city, its monuments and archaeological sites,

holy places, architecture, parks, and gardens. When I was elected mayor of Jerusalem for the first time in 1965, it was my heartfelt wish that this unique city, which has a special importance for millions of people around the world, should once again flourish and prosper, as befits its significance and grandeur.

A green and pleasant city

During our War of Independence, Jerusalem was divided for the first time in its history, and when it was reunited in 1967, our municipality had to take care of a very long list of problems and tasks. Under Jordanian rule, the city's eastern sector had been badly neglected. Its historical and religious heritage had to be preserved, and its appearance needed much improvement.

In the years which followed, more than 150 public parks and gardens were created, often with the help of

Right: The Old City and Mount of Olives from the Church of the Holy Sepulchre.

friends abroad, giving Jerusalem many lush, green spaces to be enjoyed by both residents and visitors. The large parks in the center of modern Jerusalem, the green belt surrounding the Old City's ancient stone wall, the Jerusalem Botanical Garden, the Clore Hill Garden, the Walter and Elise Haas Promenade, and the Sherover Promenade, the Koret Park, the Liberty Bell Garden, and the Wohl Rose Garden—to name just a few—all add tremendously to Jerusalem's beauty and provide excellent opportunities for its people to enjoy their leisure in a pleasant, refreshing outdoor ambience. In addition, the creation of a large green belt surrounding the entire city is now underway.

A long and complex history

Another aspect of Jerusalem's almost mythical attractiveness can be attributed to the city's long and complex history, which goes back almost 5000 years. For the last 3000 years, as their spiritual and national center, it has been the soul of the Jewish people. It was King David who in approximately 1000 B.C., turned what had been a Jebusite town into the capital of the Jewish kingdom and the religious center of Jewry—which it has remained throughout the centuries until the present.

David's son and successor, King Solomon, built the first Temple as well as his magnificent palace and also developed political and commercial ties far beyond the borders of the land of Israel. A rich spiritual and cultural life unfolded during Solomon's reign, and he continued the tradition of his psalm-composing father; various biblical books and psalms are attributed to him.

The first Temple was destroyed in 587 B.C., when Nebuchadnezzar conquered Jerusalem and deported most of its population. But the Jewish people do not easily give up, and, upon their return from the Babylonian exile some fifty years later, under the rule of the Persian king Cyrus, the second Temple was built. The city was conquered again by Alexander the Great in 332 B.C., and the subsequent attempts at Hellenization led to the Maccabean revolt in 167 B.C. Herod the Great, of the Maccabean dynasty, once more rebuilt the Temple, his structure being regarded as one of the great monuments of the age.

Following the occupation of the country by the Romans, Herod's Temple was destroyed again in 70 A.D. After the Romans, the Byzantines came and went, followed in 636 A.D., by the Arab Muslims, who built the Dome of the Rock—often regarded as one of the most beautiful buildings in the world. The Arabs, in turn, lost the city to the Crusaders in 1099 A.D., and Salah ad-Din (Saladin) regained it in 1187 A.D. In 1517 the city fell under Turkish rule, which was ended by the British exactly 400 years later during World War I.

During all these turbulent

Right: Map of Jerusalem, published in Basle, Switzerland, in 1544.

Left: A modern photograph of Jerusalem from the Mount of Olives, taking a similar viewpoint to the sixteenth-century engraving below.

Right: Aerial view of the Temple Mount area, Jerusalem. The Jewish Temple once stood on this site, now occupied by the Muslim Dome of the Rock.

centuries, Jerusalem almost always retained a Jewish population, and remained the heart and soul of Jewish people all over the world. During the War of Independence in 1948-49, Jerusalem was once again heavily fought over. When the dust settled, Jerusalem was divided between Jordan and Israel, and the Israeli part became the capital of the new Jewish state. Since 1967, Jerusalem has been united again, and the scars of a divided city are slowly disappearing.

Hidden traces

The prophets often compared Jerusalem with a beautiful woman—though the countless strangers who conquered her could keep her only for short periods. But all the invaders left traces of their presence, many still mysteriously hidden underground. Other traces have for centuries formed the city's most remarkable archaeological and architectural landmarks, especially in the Old City, which measures barely one square kilometer and is the heart of Jerusalem.

It is in the Old City that the city's unique and complex history is most evident. The Western Wall, the only major remnant of the Jewish Temple, is its focal point; nearby, part of the original City of David has been excavated and is being transformed into a wonderful archaeological park. Above it, the magnificent Muslim Dome of the Rock can be admired, having been erected where once the Temple's Holy of Holies was situated. The neighboring Jewish, Christian, Muslim, and Armenian Quarters contain innumerable houses of prayer— synagogues and *Yeshivot* (houses of Jewish study), mosques, churches, and monasteries. This religious microcosm is surrounded by the thick, imposing walls dating from the Turkish period, and built on foundations laid by Herod the Great.

This marvelous microcosm reflects Jerusalem's spiritual and religious significance to its people and to the peoples of the world, and also reflects its heterogeneous population. Here, all sorts of people live side by side: observant and secular Jews, Muslim and Christian Arabs, as well as European, Armenian, and Ethiopian Christians, Catholics, and Protestants representing a total of thirty-nine Christian denominations. In Jerusalem, Western culture and the Oriental way of life meet, coexist, cooperate, sometimes rub each other the wrong way, and finally melt together to create Jerusalem's special allure.

The Jewish majority of Jerusalem's inhabitants (coming from more than

Right: The Church of the Holy Sepulchre viewed from the south, with the garden of the Convent of St. John in the foreground. This photograph was taken in 1861 by Father Yesayi, an Armenian priest who later became Patriarch.

Left: The Jewish Quarter of Jerusalem, with the Hurva Synagogue top right, as it appeared before 1939.

Opposite: Siloam, or Hezekiah's Tunnel, part of an underground water system beneath Jerusalem built by King Hezekiah at the end of the eighth century B.C.

Right: Archaeological excavations in the City of David Archaeological Garden.

one hundred different cultural backgrounds, and speaking almost as many languages), the Arab population in East Jerusalem, and the numerous Christian groups—all have a right to preserve their traditions, culture, religion, and their ethnic way of life. Social differences, religious controversies, and ethnic and political tensions find their expression. In the city of Solomon, constant effort is needed to deal out justice to them all.

Restoration

The restoration of the Old City offers an impressive example of the fruits of our efforts. The decayed infrastructure and innumerable run-down and dangerous buildings in the Muslim, Christian, Armenian, and Jewish Quarters had to be completely renovated. Above all, the Jewish Quarter with its fifty-eight synagogues—which had been destroyed or desecrated under Jordanian rule—needed special attention and has been beautifully restored.

In 1967 only ten percent of all Old City households had running water, and sewage trickled through the corroded century-old Turkish sewers, causing extremely serious health hazards. Television aerials and electric cables—where they existed—were incompetently installed and often left dangling dangerously. Today thousands of meters of new pipes and cables and comprehensive water and electricity supply systems, as well as telephone and television cable networks, have been established. The quality of life in the Old City has been brought up to twentieth-century standards,

The peace of Jerusalem

I was glad when they said unto me,
Let us go into the house of the LORD.
Our feet shall stand within thy gates, O
Jerusalem.
Jerusalem is builded as a city that is compact
together:
Whither the tribes go up, the tribes of the
LORD, unto the testimony of Israel, to give
thanks unto the name of the LORD.
For there are set thrones of judgment,
the thrones of the house of David.
Pray for the peace of Jerusalem:
they shall prosper that love thee.
Peace be within thy walls,
and prosperity within thy palaces.
For my brethren and companions' sakes,
I will now say, Peace be within thee.
Because of the house of the LORD our God I
will seek thy good.

Psalm 122

Above: Tombs of the Sanhedrin, or Judges, in northwest Jerusalem.

Right: Exterior of the Tombs of the Sanhedrin, or Judges.

although severe overcrowding remains, especially in the Muslim Quarter. It was also especially important to supply the Arab neighborhoods outside the Old City with the same public services as the Jewish communities. In both the Jewish and the Arab sectors, schools and kindergartens, community centers, senior citizens' homes, clinics, and museums have been built, and a wide range of popular joint Arab-Jewish cultural programs are carried out every year by the Jerusalem Foundation.

Above: The Tombs of the Kings, identified as the tomb of Queen Adiabene, died c. 65 A.D.

Cultural life

Cultural life in Jerusalem offers a great variety of choices. The Israel Museum presents, in addition to changing exhibitions, excellent permanent archaeological collections featuring Bible lands, as well as fine examples of art from the Old Masters, modern art and sculpture, Jewish ceremonial art, and good examples of art created all over the world in every period until today. In the adjacent Shrine of the Book, the Dead Sea Scrolls can be admired. A magnificent new addition to Jerusalem's museums is the Museum of the History of Jerusalem, which occupies David's Tower—the Citadel integrated into the Old City walls at the Jaffa Gate. Exquisite archaeological finds can also be enjoyed at the Rockefeller Museum.

Every two years the Jerusalem International Book Fair attracts hundreds of foreign publishers, writers, and booksellers and represents Israel's focal point for the interchange of literature of international significance. Each spring the Israel Festival—one of Israel's major cultural events—draws visitors to Jerusalem from all over Israel and the world. Hundreds of artists from many nations gather in Jerusalem to enchant the public with theater, mime, concerts, ballet, puppet shows, and much more.

Right: Jews at the
Western Wall before the
1967 war.

City of light

Jerusalem's architecture adds greatly
to its beauty both because of the
contrasting building styles of
different periods and because of the
predominant building material, the
famous white Jerusalem stone which
reflects the sunlight—one of the
reasons Jerusalem is called the "City
of Light." A law passed by the
British during the pre-World War II
Mandate demanded that every new
building in Jerusalem be built with
this local limestone.

Since this was a good idea, we kept
it this way, and new, modern
buildings fit splendidly into the
cityscape. The Sheikh Jarrah Health
Care Center in East Jerusalem, the
Mamilla project (a new residential
area next to the Old City), the
Mormons' Brigham Young
University, the new Supreme Court,
and of course, the new City Hall—to
name just a few—are exceptional
examples of aesthetically pleasing
and functional modern buildings
perfectly in harmony with tradition.
The new City Hall, next to the Jaffa
Gate, is situated on the divide
between old and new Jerusalem and
now centralizes all the offices of the
municipal and district authorities
which were previously scattered
around town. The key architectural
element is a sequence of three public
squares that create a focus of activity
at all hours of day and evening.

Jerusalem's predominant

industries are metal, food,
pharmaceuticals, and publishing. In
addition to the commercial and
industrial centers in the Talpiot and
Giv'at Sha'ul neighborhoods, the
Jerusalem Development Authority
(JDA) plans an industrial park for

high-tech companies in southwestern Jerusalem. The JDA was
founded in 1989 by the government
and the municipality, and its
activities are aimed at utilizing the
highly educated manpower available
in Jerusalem and preserving the

Right: Jews at the Western Wall before the 1967 war.

Below: The Jewish
Quarter in the eighteenth
century; a French
illustration.

city's human and physical landscape. To date, the JDA has initiated and completed nearly fifty large urban projects. Entrepreneurs are beginning to move to Jerusalem; construction, trade, industry, and tourism are all on the increase.

A complex city

Against the background of its great historic, cultural, and religious importance, Jerusalem is a complex modern city with a very heterogeneous population, and the serious difficulties this sometimes causes cannot be solved quickly. The results of our efforts are not always immediately obvious. And, as New York's former mayor Ed Koch has stated, Jerusalem is the world's most difficult city to govern. But our policy of taking small steps over almost three decades and of promoting democracy and tolerance have indeed proven themselves, especially during the years of the *Intifada*, during which Jerusalem remained relatively calm and the cooperation of the city's Arab employees continued.

Integration of the Arab population into city life has worked well. About ten years ago, in parts of the city we started creating Arab and Jewish district administrations with authority in all local decisions, such as school registration, cultural matters, and some building activities. This successful idea should be implemented gradually throughout the city.

Jerusalem and its people have

Left: Jerusalem from the Mount of Olives.

Below: Panorama of Jerusalem from the Mount of Olives, taken in 1870. The Dome of the Rock and the Golden Gate feature prominently.

Previous spread: Israeli
soldiers celebrate the
recapture of Jerusalem at
the Western Wall in 1967.
Among them is Rabbi
Shlomo Goren.

Opposite: An Orthodox
Jew copies the *Torah*.

Right: An Israeli soldier
at the Western Wall.

Right: Reconstructed arch of the Hurva Synagogue, which stands on the ruins of the Crusader Church of St. Martin in the Jewish Quarter.

Right: A seven-branched candlestick, frequently a symbol of Israel.

good reason to be proud of their achievements. There is freedom of movement, freedom of religion, with free access to the holy sites, for the first time in history. Jerusalem will continue to be an open, pluralistic city for everybody. It will take time to solve all the problems, but it is still better to live in a united city with difficulties than to live in a divided city.

This splendid book is an important contribution to Jerusalem's celebration of its 3000-year birthday as the Jewish capital. It shows you Jerusalem's beauty, its history, its people and their lives; the brilliant photographs by Hilla and Max-Moshe Jacoby speak for themselves. Enjoy your photographic visit to Jerusalem, and hopefully you will be inspired to visit in person—Next Year in Jerusalem!

Teddy Kollek

2

The Story of Jerusalem

"The LORD is great in Zion;
and he is high above all the people."
(Psalm 99:2)

The Hills of Moab.

Opposite: Jerusalem from the surrounding hills.

Early years

For three millennia, the history of Jerusalem has been shaped by its importance as the national and spiritual center of the Jewish people. Jerusalem is mentioned in the Bible over 600 times and in the daily Jewish prayers, and also bears almost equal significance as a holy city for both Christians and Muslims all over the world.

The city's unique geographical location at the crossroads of the spheres of influence of the ancient empires of the region—Egypt, Assyria, Babylon, Persia, Greece, Rome, Byzantium, as well as the Arabs and Turks—constantly exposed it to the perils of war, conquest, and destruction. Periods of stability and prosperity alternated with times of conflict and upheaval.

But ever since the time of David, when Jerusalem became the center of Jewish life, there has been a Jewish

Below: The Old City viewed from the Mount of Olives. The city walls and Temple Mount area are clearly visible.

Salem

And Melchizedek king of Salem brought forth bread and wine: and he was the priest of the most high God. And he blessed him, and said, Blessed be Abram of the most high God, possessor of heaven and earth: and blessed be the most high God, which hath delivered thine enemies into thy hand.
Genesis 14:18-20

presence in the city—except for a short time following the expulsion of the Jews by the Romans and during the Crusader period, when Jews were forbidden to live in the city. Since the mid-nineteenth century, the majority of Jerusalem's population has been Jewish, and in 1948 the city was once again proclaimed the political capital of Israel, at the center of an independent, modern, democratic Jewish state.

Earliest evidence

Jerusalem's history reaches back further almost than the memory of humankind. The earliest traces of human settlement on the site of Jerusalem date back nearly 5000 years, and are found around the Gihon Spring, and can still be seen today. They include the remains of the settlement's ancient water system. Without this spring,

Previous spread: Jerusalem at dusk.

Previous spread (inset): Full moon over Mount Zion. The moon rises between the towers of the Dormition Church and the Church of the Holy Saviour.

Opposite: The Mount of Olives from the walls of the Old City. A large cemetery is situated on the slopes of the mount.

Below: The Mount of Olives.

Jerusalem would never have developed into the important political and economic metropolis that played such a major role in the history of the ancient Middle East. Situated in the Kidron Valley to the southeast of today's modern city, the Gihon Spring provides water throughout the year, even in the dry months of spring, summer, and early autumn, and thus provides one indispensable prerequisite for human settlement.

Archaeological finds south of the spring supply evidence for the presence of early settlers in the area. Pieces of excavated pottery were manufactured by shepherds who found shelter in nearby caves and tents. They left this site sometime around the beginning of the third millennium B.C., probably because their flocks could no longer be sustained on the sparse foliage near the spring.

First written record
For almost the next 1000 years, the site appears to have remained deserted, until about 2000 B.C. Finds of pottery and the remains of graves from the Early Bronze Age show that, once again, people had settled around the Gihon Spring. By that time, Egypt held supremacy over the region. The first written reference to Jerusalem, dating from the

Mount Zion

*They that trust in the L*ORD *shall be as mount Zion,*
which cannot be removed, but abideth for ever.
As the mountains are round about Jerusalem,
*so the L*ORD *is round about his people from*
henceforth even for ever.
For the rod of the wicked shall not rest upon the lot
of the righteous;
lest the righteous put forth their hands unto
iniquity.
*Do good, O L*ORD, *unto those that be good,*
and to them that are upright in their hearts.
Psalm 125:1-4

Opposite: The Temple Mount from the lower slopes of the Mount of Olives. The Garden of Gethsemane is situated among the trees at the foot of the hill.

Right: The Temple Mount and Old City from the Mount of Olives. Part of the extensive Jewish cemetery is in the foreground; many Jews wish to be buried in Jerusalem.

fourteenth century B.C., was unearthed at the site of Tel el-Amarna in Egypt; Jerusalem is named as one of the towns that paid tribute to Egypt. But evidence is scant, and not much can be determined about the settlement which was later to become Jerusalem.

Overrun by the mysterious Hyksos people in the eighteenth century B.C., the Egyptian Empire lost its influence in the land of Canaan, and the city-states of the region became more independent. At the same time, migration to the region by peoples from the east—among them the forefathers of the Hebrews—as well as from the west (the Philistines) increased Jerusalem's early exposure to the outside world.

The settlement was now transformed from a remote village in the Kidron Valley to a fortified town along the western slope of the valley, below the site of modern Jerusalem. Water from the spring was carried up to the town. While this arrangement was satisfactory during peacetime, the settlement could all too easily be cut off from its water supply in times of unrest and war. Around 1500 B.C., this problem was resolved by the digging of a tunnel from within the town walls. A flight of stone steps was constructed leading down to the spring, enabling the inhabitants to get their water without being exposed to attack.

The history of the ancient Middle East is generally characterized by repeated waves of migration by nomadic tribes and peoples looking for literally greener pastures. Such groups usually clashed with the inhabitants of the city-states and settlements they encountered, and which the nomads often conquered and subsequently settled, absorbing the remnants of the earlier populations. The arrival of the people of Israel in the area should be viewed within this context.

Exodus
The story of the Hebrew people's exodus from Egypt into the Promised Land is one of the most significant stories in the Bible. The Hebrews migrated to this region, advancing west and north, attacking and at times destroying existing settlements. The well-known story of the fall of Jericho is just one example of this process. For the people of Israel, there was a gradual transition from a nomadic life, a slow process of settling the land. At first, Jerusalem did not attract the attention of the newcomers, being a comparatively small and unimportant town.

From judges to kings
The need of the twelve tribes of Israel for more centralized organization, more suitable than the existing loose association, soon evolved. The people, probably in imitation of what they saw in other political entities around them, demanded a king. Thus the leadership by elders and judges ended, and Saul was anointed the first king of Israel.

The process of becoming a nation and forming a state was difficult, and in the end it was David who showed greater leadership qualities than Saul. David and Saul had earlier been close friends—David married Saul's daughter—but the growing rivalry between the two men eventually led to Saul's utter hostility toward David, who spent several years fleeing Saul.

Following Saul's death, David eventually defeated Saul's son Ishbosheth and succeeded him, uniting the people of Israel and forging them into a nation. When the year-long civil war between his followers and those of Saul's son was resolved, David was proclaimed king over all Israel. He was still only thirty years old. For seven years, it is reported, he continued ruling from his capital of Hebron; but this city traditionally represented the center of power of the tribe of Judah—a fact which apparently impeded the integration of the twelve tribes of Israel and the consolidation of a Jewish state.

David chooses Jerusalem
Jerusalem, by this time an independent city-state, had distanced itself from the skirmishes and battles between the Jews and the Philistines. The city had avoided war and

conquest by strictly preserving its neutrality. For the same reason it took no part in the tribal rivalries between the northern and southern areas of Jewish settlement. David therefore chose Jerusalem for its political suitability, as well as its ideal geographic location between the two blocs of Jewish clans.

By the time David marched against Jerusalem in 1006 B.C., the city was inhabited by the Jebusites, one of the Canaanite peoples who had previously given up the nomadic lifestyle. The tunnel leading from within the city to the Gihon Spring outside the walls was the city's weakest point. One of David's soldiers succeeded in entering the city via this tunnel and opened Jerusalem's gates for David and his men.

David made Jerusalem the capital of the kingdom of Israel and the

Opposite: The Tomb of Absalom in the Kidron Valley, on the east side of the city. Falsely named, the tomb probably dates from the first century A.D., and belonged to a wealthy Jewish family.

Right: The Tomb of Absalom from the rear.

home of the one God. He refrained from killing the city's indigenous population and, with the help of the city's experts, he succeeded in turning Jerusalem into the administrative and political center of the Jewish state. He extended his power far to the north and the east, while continuing to prevent the Philistines from crossing Israel's western borders. David's victories changed the balance of power in the Middle East; helped by the decline of Egypt, he transformed Jerusalem into a power center to be reckoned with in the region.

The spiritual significance of his new capital was symbolized when David moved the Ark of the Covenant into the city—an act that made Jerusalem the center of worship for the people of Israel and a place of pilgrimage from all parts of the land. But plans to build a permanent home for the Ark—a Temple—were not realized during David's lifetime. David, as a warrior, had blood on his hands, which, according to religious law, prohibited him from building the sanctuary.

Solomon and the first Temple

It was Solomon, David's son and successor, who completed the task by building the first Temple in Jerusalem. Building materials and artisans were brought in from Lebanon. Solomon extended the administration his father had built, using it mainly to recruit armies from all parts of the land, and introduced a new tax-collection system. The city had grown rapidly

Below: The tombs of Bene Hezir (left) and of Zechariah in the Kidron Valley.

Opposite: The golden domes of the Russian Orthodox Church of St. Mary Magdalene at Gethsemane.

in size and population, and the new king needed funds for his extensive construction projects. The water supply was improved by building a channel leading from the Gihon Spring to a small pool about 300 meters (980 feet) away, creating a water reservoir urgently needed by Jerusalem's growing population.

The reign of King Solomon is remembered mainly as a period of prosperity and growth. Political and commercial ties were extended, and new trade routes developed. The new shipyard in the town of Ezion-Geber, on the Gulf of Eilat, produced seaworthy ships and provided the harbor from which they sailed and to which they returned with their cargoes. A new social structure also developed—the affluent and the noble clustered around the Temple and the magnificent new palace built by Solomon, while the poor remained below, in the original city of David. It was mainly from these poorer strata of the people that Solomon recruited forced labor for his ambitious construction projects. The unceasing efforts of thousands of these laborers are among the less-pleasant aspects of his rule.

Right: The Golden Gate (*Bab al-Dhahabi*) in the city wall. Many Christians believe that Jesus will enter this gate at his Second Coming.

Opposite: Interior of the Citadel of Jerusalem, situated on one of the highest parts of the Old City. Now the Museum of the History of Jerusalem, it is probably the site of the Praetorium, where Jesus was condemned to death.

The Citadel

The kingdom divides

Solomon reigned over the kingdom for forty years, and upon his death in 928 B.C., the old grievances between the north and south surfaced once again. The kingdom divided, with Jerusalem remaining the capital of Judah in the south, ruled by Solomon's son Rehoboam.

The message that emanated from Jerusalem over the next centuries was to shape the history of mankind. It was in this period and during the Babylonian exile that Isaiah, Jeremiah, and other prophets in the city called for social justice, equity, and faith. The northern kingdom of Israel was ruled by Jeroboam, one of Solomon's former nobles. Jeroboam set up a rival sanctuary at Beth-El, about 30 kilometers (18 miles) north of Jerusalem, but many of his subjects still continued their pilgrimage to Jerusalem three times a year for the feasts of *Pesach* (Passover), *Shavuot* (Pentecost), and *Succoth* (Tabernacles).

The division of the kingdom weakened the overall power of the Jewish nation. Just a few years later Jerusalem, and subsequently the northern kingdom as well, were raided by an Egyptian army. A period of civil war between Judah and Israel followed, and the rift between the two states deepened. Jerusalem's importance as a political and military center of power diminished, and the city became a less important, almost provincial town. David's dynasty continued to rule in Jerusalem, but no outstanding leading personality emerged. Over the next 300 years, many kings came and went.

The First Exile

In the eighth century B.C., the Assyrian Empire gained considerable influence in the region. Attempts by the smaller nations and city-states to withstand the pressure failed, and Assyrian conquests proceeded inexorably. In 722 B.C., the kingdom of Israel fell and became an Assyrian province. The elite, nobility, and priests were deported to Mesopotamia in what is known as the First Exile.

But like all the other great ancient empires, Assyria was also bound to decline. When Josiah became king of Judah in 639 B.C., Assyrian power

Right: The Citadel viewed from outside the city walls.

The City of David

David was thirty years old when he began to reign, and he reigned forty years. In Hebron he reigned over Judah seven years and six months: and in Jerusalem he reigned thirty and three years over all Israel and Judah. And the king and his men went to Jerusalem unto the Jebusites, the inhabitants of the land: which spake unto David, saying, Except thou take away the blind and the lame, thou shalt not come in hither: thinking, David cannot come in hither. Nevertheless David took the stronghold of Zion: the same is the city of David. . . . So David dwelt in the fort, and called it the city of David. And David built round about from Millo and inward. And David went on, and grew great, and the LORD God of hosts was with him.

2 Samuel 5:4-7,9,10

Opposite: Part of the Citadel.

had already begun to fade, and the newly emerging Babylon had not yet exercised any perceptible influence in the land of Israel. Sensing an opportunity for greater independence, Josiah tried to renew the covenant with the one God, and to reunite the heartlands of the Jewish people.

When in 609 B.C. the Assyrian king invoked his pact with Egypt to request aid in his crusade against Babylon, an Egyptian army passed through Israel. Josiah inclined to support Babylon, since alliance with this faraway power might have ensured him greater freedom than alliance with nearby Egypt. Accordingly, he sent an army to repel the passing Egyptian forces. The Judeans were defeated in a battle north of Jerusalem, and Josiah was killed. For the next years Jerusalem and Judah were controlled by Egypt; the attempt to reestablish an independent Jewish state had miserably failed.

The continuing power struggle between Babylon and Egypt was finally resolved by a Babylonian victory over Egypt. The entire area between the Fertile Crescent in the east and Egypt in the west fell to the Babylonian king, Nebuchadnezzar. Josiah's son, Jehoiakim, failed to understand that the balance of power had shifted; he ignored the warnings of the prophet Jeremiah and declared his loyalty to Egypt.

Right: Part of the Citadel, occupied successively by the Romans, Crusaders, Mameluks, and Ottomans.

Right: A round tower in the Citadel.

Opposite: The massive masonry of the Citadel, known in Crusader times as the Tower of David.

Left: Interior of the Citadel of Jerusalem; remains dating from many different periods have been discovered within its walls.

Opposite: Part of the restored Ottoman stonework of the Jaffa Gate.

Right: These lions or panthers dating from Suleiman II's time are found on St. Stephen's Gate, traditional site of the saint's martyrdom.

Below: An Israeli soldier guards the Jaffa Gate, entered by Allenby and the British army in 1917.

When subsequently Nebuchadnezzar attacked Jerusalem, Jehoiakim died during the siege, and his son and successor Jehoiachin had no choice but to capitulate.

The Second Exile

Although robbed of its treasures, Jerusalem was not destroyed. Unfortunately, however, Jehoiachin's successor, Zedekiah, who was crowned by the Babylonians, repeated Jehoiakim's mistake of underestimating the strength of Babylon's hegemony. His attempted revolt was countered by a Babylonian army marching against Jerusalem and conquering it after a prolonged siege, in 587 B.C.

The city was destroyed, the walls torn down, and the Temple burned. More than half the population was exiled to Babylon, with only the poorer inhabitants left in Judah under a governor appointed by Nebuchadnezzar. The Second Exile brought an end to the 400-year "First Temple Period."

Historians have asked themselves many times if this catastrophe was

Opposite: The Montefiore Windmill, facing Mount Zion, was built in the nineteenth century by the Anglo-Jewish philanthropist Sir Moses Montefiore.

inevitable. At the time it certainly must have been very difficult for the kings in Jerusalem to judge the situation correctly and to decide which of the great powers would eventually gain the upper hand. Such a dilemma repeats itself throughout Jerusalem's history.

The exile of the Jewish people by the rivers of Babylon continued for almost fifty years before they were allowed to return to their homeland—historically speaking, a very short period. Nevertheless, the shock of mass expulsion, together with the destruction of their city, and above all of the Temple, left a permanent, deep, and painful impression in the memory of the Jewish people.

The Second Temple

In 538 B.C., Babylon was conquered by King Cyrus of Persia. That same year this tolerant king issued a decree permitting the Jews to return to Jerusalem. The Persian ruler allowed the Jewish people to rebuild the Temple, perform sacrifices, and practice their faith—a concession which was upheld by Cyrus' successors, Darius and Artaxerxes.

In 516 B.C., the second Temple was consecrated. But political independence for Judah was out of the question. Cyrus forbade the refortification of the city walls and

Below: (left to right) The Montefiore Windmill, Sheraton Hotel, YMCA, and King David Hotel, viewed from outside the city walls.

A quiet habitation

Look upon Zion, the city of our solemnities: thine eyes shall see Jerusalem a quiet habitation, a tabernacle that shall not be taken down; not one of the stakes thereof shall ever be removed, neither shall any of the cords thereof be broken. But there the glorious LORD will be unto us a place of broad rivers and streams; wherein shall go no galley with oars, neither shall gallant ship pass thereby. For the LORD is our judge, the LORD is our lawgiver, the LORD is our king; he will save us. Thy tacklings are loosed; they could not well strengthen their mast, they could not spread the sail: then is the prey of a great spoil divided; the lame take the prey. And the inhabitant shall not say, I am sick: the people that dwell therein shall be forgiven their iniquity.

Isaiah 33:20-24

the restoration of a Jewish monarchy in Jerusalem. Political power lay in the hands of the Persian satrap, installed to rule over what was now no more than a Persian province.

A period of peace ensued and, since there was no possibility of the Jewish people freeing themselves from the Persian yoke, other aspects

of their national identity gained significance. In Jerusalem and the surrounding lands, religious, cultural, social, and economic life developed under Ezra and Nehemiah, two prominent Jewish leaders who had arrived from Babylon to help reconstruct Jewish life in the Jewish land.

Above: The Arab *souk* in the Old City.

Jerusalem and its Temple were not fully restored to their former glory, and Ezra imposed a very strict interpretation of the religious law. But in internal matters the Jews gained a certain autonomy under Persian sovereignty, and were once more united as a nation. Jerusalem became a city of peace, and Jews from all over the Persian Empire continued to make annual pilgrimages to the center of their faith.

Hellenization

In 334 B.C., Alexander the Great marched against Persia, defeating the Persian armies at Issos in 333 B.C. One year later his army conquered Judah and Jerusalem. However, the status of the Jews did not change under Macedonian rule; Alexander allowed them to continue living according to the customs of their forefathers. Jerusalem did not attract Alexander's attention; to him it must have appeared just another small city among the many that fell to him, and the legend about his visit to the city holds no truth.

Although religious freedom was granted, Greek rule brought something else: Hellenism. Greek language and culture took hold throughout the vast empire conquered by Alexander, spread by his armies and administrators, and by the merchants and settlers who followed them. Characterized by a pronounced emphasis on the individual and a more material approach to life, this culture offered a totally different climate to that which had been reestablished and strengthened by Ezra and Nehemiah. In Jerusalem, as in all the cities of the new empire, a gradual process of Hellenization began.

After Alexander's death in 323 B.C., his empire disintegrated and his successors fought over it. In 320 B.C., Judah was invaded by Ptolemy, who now ruled Egypt. During the following century, Judah, and with it Jerusalem, suffered from the dispute between the Seleucids ruling in the northeast over greater Syria, and the Ptolemies of Egypt. Again the land of Israel was torn between two great centers of power until in 199 B.C. the Seleucid hegemony was established.

Jerusalem prospers

Under Hellenistic influence, commerce and trade became major sources of income for the citizens of Jerusalem, enabling the city to expand. New streets were constructed in a grid pattern, making traffic much easier. The expansion of trade brought with it an increase in travel and a new social order; wealth was no longer concentrated in the hands of a small, elite group, but began to be distributed among a larger proportion of the population. Greek became the lingua franca of the entire region.

Naturally, a large part of Jerusalem's establishment opposed these new developments, wanting to preserve the status quo. Others, who had developed strong personal ties with the Greek authorities, favored the adoption of Greek customs. Consequently, by the time Antiochus III came to power in 190 B.C., two main factions had developed among Jerusalem's citizens: pro-Hellenists opposed the conservative residents who advocated stricter adherence to Jewish law and lifestyle.

Antiochus III renewed the granting of freedom of religion, recognizing the Jewish high priest and the Council of Elders as the representatives of Jerusalem and Judah. It was under Antiochus III's successor, Antiochus IV (Epiphanes), that things began to change drastically. Across the Mediterranean, Rome had—almost unnoticed—begun to rise, and Antiochus IV was increasingly aware of the threat posed by this new emerging power. It is likely that he wanted to consolidate his empire and strengthen his hold over it by

enforcing conformity in religion.

Antiochus IV backed the Hellenistic faction in Jerusalem, and subsequently ordered that the Temple of the one God be consecrated to Zeus. This desecration, paired with Antiochus IV's plundering of the Temple's treasury, led to a rebellion in Jerusalem that he swiftly crushed. Even stronger measures were now decreed; Antiochus forbade the Jews to practice their religion or follow its laws. Jerusalem had been turned into a Greek city-state.

The Maccabean Wars

In 167 B.C., an attempt by a group of soldiers to enforce the new religious laws in the Judean village of Modi'in caused a riot that quickly developed into a revolt, headed by the family of Mattathiah and his five sons. The rebellion rapidly gained momentum, led after Mattathiah's death by his son Judas, whose epithet "Macca-beus" (the Hammer) gave the uprising its name.

Following two years of relentless guerrilla war against Antiochus IV and the Hellenistic Jewish group which ruled as his vassals, the Maccabeans occupied Jerusalem and restored the Temple—an event still commemorated by the Jewish people and celebrated every year with the feast of Hanukkah (Dedication).

The wars of the Maccabeans continued, but eventually the power of the Seleucid Empire weakened. In 141 B.C., Judas' brother Simon proclaimed the independent state of Judah and, after four centuries of foreign rule, Jerusalem once again became the residence of a Jewish king.

Simon founded the Hasmonean dynasty, which ruled in Jerusalem for about eighty years, until internal strife precipitated Roman rule. Two contenders for the crown—the Hasmonean brothers Hyrcanus and Aristobulus—engaged in a bloody civil war. When Hyrcanus lost, he called upon Rome for support. Pompey conquered Jerusalem in 63 B.C., Judah becoming a Roman protectorate, and Rome governing Jerusalem.

Twenty-six years later, Herod, a Roman protégé of Idumean origin, made Jerusalem his capital and transformed it into one of the most beautiful cities of the world. Its centerpiece was the Temple, which he enlarged and embellished. Herod bore the title of king, but was no more than a Roman vassal. The Christian world remembers him as the legendary villain who ordered the child Jesus killed, fearing for his position as king of the Jews. Ten years after Herod's death and following the unsuccessful reign of his heir, direct Roman rule was restored. It was during this period that Jesus of Nazareth was preaching in the city.

The Jewish revolt

The Jewish people never accepted their loss of independence, and during the reign of Emperor Titus in 70 A.D., a Jewish revolt against the Romans ended in the destruction of Jerusalem and the second Temple. Another Jewish revolt broke out during the reign of Emperor Hadrian in 132 A.D., led by Simon Bar Kochba.

For a short time, Jerusalem was restored as the Jewish capital, but in 135 A.D., the Romans crushed this revolt too. A massive, systematic deportation drastically reduced Jerusalem's Jewish population, and Hadrian rebuilt Jerusalem as a Roman city, naming it Aelia Capitolina. Jerusalem and Judah were now fully incorporated into the growing Roman Empire; Jerusalem no longer existed as a Jewish capital.

"Next year in Jerusalem"

Due to the depopulation of Jerusalem and Judah by Rome, a large-scale dispersion of the Jewish people throughout the Roman Empire began. Jewish traders traveled the Roman roads and built Jewish communities all over the Levant and Europe. The Jews of the Diaspora (Dispersion) never forgot Jerusalem and never lost their hope to return someday. Their longing was expressed in their prayers, such as those during the feast of *Pesach* (Passover), which concluded with the words: "Next year in Jerusalem."

Above: The southern wall of the city, climbing to Mount Zion to the left.

Christian holy places

Jerusalem once more underwent change, after the the conversion of the Emperor Constantine to Christianity, in 312, and his subsequent favouring of the church. By this time Jerusalem was no longer the administrative capital of Judah (the Roman province of Judea); this honor had been bestowed on Caesarea Maritima, on the Mediterranean coast northwest of Jerusalem. But in view of its importance to Christianity and to its founder, Jerusalem became one of the region's episcopal sees, and Constantine ordered the erection of monuments at the Christian holy places in the city as well as the construction of hostels to accommodate the influx of pilgrims.

Constantine's mother, Helena, visited Jerusalem in 326 A.D., initiating the construction of a number of churches, among them the Church of the Holy Sepulchre. The Roman name of Aelia Capitolina was abandoned, and Jerusalem was once more called by its proper name.

Under Constantine, Jerusalem's Jewish population increased in number, and his successor, Julian, even gave permission to rebuild the Jewish Temple. However, his decree remained a dead letter since Julian remained in power for only a short time, and his permission was revoked by his successor.

Muslim supremacy

In the seventh century, the Christians gave way to the Muslims. The Byzantine Christian armies were protected by heavy coats of mail, which hindered their mobility against the quick Arab horsemen, and by 638 A.D. they had no choice but to surrender Jerusalem to Caliph Omar Ibn el-Khatab after being defeated in a battle southwest of the city.

Within two years the Islamic state had spread throughout the Middle East. The many similarities between the Old Testament and the *Qur'an* can be traced to the close contacts Muhammad and his early followers had with Jewish communities in Arabia. The Muslims granted Jerusalem's Jewish and Christian populations freedom of religion, but in order to reinforce Muslim supremacy they were made second-class citizens.

Muslim shrines

Under the Muslims, the Dome of the Rock, the Aqsa Mosque, and many other Muslim shrines were constructed, making Jerusalem the third holiest city in Islam. Before Mecca became the required direction of prayer (*kibla*), the prophet Muhammad instructed the devout to pray towards Jerusalem, since it was considered to be the gateway to paradise. In Muslim tradition, Jerusalem is also the city of the farthest mosque—El Aqsa—to which Muhammad traveled on his legendary Night Journey, and the place from which he ascended to heaven.

For more than four centuries Muslim rule continued, periods of comparative religious and cultural freedom for Jerusalem's inhabitants alternating with times of stricter Islamic rule, and even the oppression of Jews and Christians.

The Crusades

Towards the end of the eleventh century, the Muslims introduced severe restrictions concerning the access of pilgrims to the Christian holy places. In faraway Europe, Pope Urban II called upon the Christian world to launch a crusade against the Muslims to free these places from the power of the "infidels." As a result, Jerusalem once again came into Christian hands in 1099 with the victory of the Crusaders. Their armies under the famous Godfrey de Bouillon conquered Jerusalem, massacring most of its population,

Right: Arab houses in the Kidron Valley.

Jews and Muslims alike. The city itself was looted and burned. After Godfrey's death the following year, his brother Baldwin proclaimed Jerusalem the capital of the Crusaders' kingdom, with himself as king.

Having made Jerusalem their headquarters, the Crusaders extended their power to Jericho in the east and Galilee in the north. Along the Mediterranean coast they conquered the rich ports of Ashkelon, Sidon, Beirut, and Tyre, and amassed great riches. But the Crusaders' Latin kingdom of

Left: The Kidron Valley, outside the walls of the Old City.

Jerusalem remained comparatively small.

The Muslim world was not willing to accept an independent Christian enclave in their midst. The Muslims never ceased to attack the Christian kingdom, but their attacks began to have an impact only when a strong leader by the name of Salah ad-Din—later known to the Western world as Sultan Saladin—took it upon himself to destroy the Crusaders' realm, expelling them in 1187. They enjoyed one further brief period in Jerusalem when, following yet another crusade led by the famous kings Richard the Lionheart of England, Frederick Barbarossa of Germany, and Philippe Auguste of France, the city was regained by a treaty with the Muslim rulers in 1229. But their time was definitely over when in 1290 the Mameluk ruler, Kalawun, drove the Crusaders out of the Holy Land for good.

Turkish Rule
By 1250 the soldier caste of the Mameluks, consisting of slaves imported mainly from Turkey, gained control over Egypt, Palestine, and Syria. Their rule paved the way for the Ottoman Turks, who in 1517 conquered the Mameluk empire and, with it, Jerusalem.

Below: Steps leading down to the Tomb of Lazarus, Bethany.

Under Turkish rule, Jerusalem regained something of its former beauty. Sultan Suleiman "the Magnificent" wanted the city refortified and gave orders to rebuild the city walls, which still stand around Jerusalem's Old City. The Turkish governors administering the Ottoman provinces granted their subjects freedom of religion, although it was difficult to gain permission to build synagogues.

Most of the approximately 200,000 Jews uprooted by the Spanish Inquisition found a new home within the Turkish Empire, and quite a few settled in Jerusalem, whose Jewish population increased considerably during the sixteenth century. Following negotiations with various European countries, Christianity was also tolerated.

Christian denominations were permitted to establish themselves, and many of today's monasteries and churches originate from this period.

However, under Turkish rule Jerusalem did not become an administrative center, and Israel was ruled from Damascus or Beirut. The city retained a rather provincial character, as is reflected in many European travelers' diaries from that time. As the Turkish Empire declined, initial religious tolerance gave way in the eighteenth, and especially the nineteenth, centuries to growing restrictions.

With the rise of Zionism towards the end of the nineteenth century, many Jewish immigrants found their way from Europe to the land of Israel. As the Jewish population

increased in number, Jews started to build new neighborhoods outside the Old City's walls. The decline of the Turkish Empire offered a new opportunity for European countries to gain a foothold in Jerusalem, and a considerable number of European consulates were established in the city. But with pilgrims providing the only substantial source of income, commerce and industry were non-existent in Jerusalem; the city was poor and almost nothing remained of its former glory. The holy sites of all three religions were neglected, buildings decayed, and living conditions generally deteriorated.

The British Mandate
This was the Jerusalem captured by Britain in 1917 during World War I. The British conquered Palestine and were given a mandate to administer it by the League of Nations. British and French interests in the Middle East and in its resources had led these two nations secretly to divide the region into areas of influence in 1915 under the Sykes-Picot agreement; Palestine was to be under British influence.

Only months after General Edmund Allenby marched into Jerusalem, the British issued the Balfour Declaration, which promised the creation of a Jewish national homeland in Palestine. The Balfour Declaration and the introduction of nation-states into the Middle East gave the Jewish people reason for the first time in 2000 years to hope for a real chance to regain their independence as a nation and to return to Jerusalem as their capital.

During the British Mandate period, Jerusalem's Jewish population tripled in number. The aspirations of the Jewish people and the rise of Arab nationalism led to many riots and numerous violent clashes between the Jewish and the Arab populations. This was especially the case in Jerusalem, where the two peoples lived comparatively crowded together, and where Arab attacks on Jews were particularly brutal.

The era of large empires was over, and in 1947, with the British about to leave Palestine, the United Nations approved a resolution that would give Jerusalem international status and divide the land between the two peoples. This resolution was rejected by the Arabs and accepted reluctantly by the Jews.

Above: The village of Bethany, with (left to right) the Franciscan Church, Mosque, and Greek Church.

The Knesset

Opposite: The Knesset viewed from the surrounding gardens.

With the end of World War II, the innumerable Jewish displaced persons in Europe needed a haven, and the United Nations resolution offered a solution without bloodshed. The international status suggested for Jerusalem was supposed to continue for a period of ten years, after which a plebiscite was to be held. Since at the time Jerusalem's Jewish population amounted to 100,000, and the Arab population to only 65,000, the Jews seemed to have a good chance of winning such a plebiscite. But the Arabs attacked Israel and war broke out.

Right: The Israel Parliament, or Knesset, at the south end of Sacher Park.

Fierce battles

Jerusalem was the site of particularly fierce battles and fell under long and agonizing months of siege; food, and especially water, became very scarce. As local tradition has it, this terrible shortage is the reason why Jerusalemites are still extremely

Below: The Knesset in session. A visitors' galley is open to the public.

sparing with water. The wrecks of Israeli vehicles which tried to break through the Arab lines with supplies can still be seen along the Jerusalem-Tel Aviv highway—left there to bear witness to those hard times.

This period of combat during

Israel's War of Independence (1948-49) ended in the division of the city of Jerusalem into two parts, namely West Jerusalem, the Israeli sector; and East Jerusalem, the Jordanian sector. Jerusalem was proclaimed the capital of the young State of Israel,

Opposite: The Pool of
Siloam.

Right: The Siloam spring,
which feeds the Pool of
Siloam.

Water

The Pool of Siloam

And as Jesus passed by, he saw a man which was blind from his birth. And his disciples asked him, saying, Master, who did sin, this man, or his parents, that he was born blind? Jesus answered, Neither hath this man sinned, nor his parents: but that the works of God should be made manifest in him. I must work the works of him that sent me, while it is day: the night cometh, when no man can work. As long as I am in the world, I am the light of the world. When he had thus spoken, he spat on the ground, and made clay of the spittle, and he anointed the eyes of the blind man with the clay, and said unto him, Go, wash in the pool of Siloam, (which is by interpretation, Sent). He went his way therefore, and washed, and came seeing.

John 9:1-7

Right: Solomon's Pools
near the Hebron Road,
for centuries a vital
reservoir for Jerusalem.

monasteries and churches, were
made accessible to all.

Today, the holy sites are governed
by their respective communities
without Israeli interference.
Extensive reconstruction has turned
the Old City into one of the most
beautiful parts of Jerusalem. And
after almost two decades, people
returned to live in the Jewish
Quarter, next to the Armenian,
Christian, and Muslim Quarters of
the Old City.

Modern Jerusalem

Today, Jerusalem has become a
modern city, providing employment
and housing for its inhabitants and
offering all the facilities of a
twentieth-century community. At
the same time, the city bears witness
to its age-old history and retains a
unique quality and mystery that
makes it precious to its inhabitants as
well as to its admirers all over the
world.

For almost thirty years, until 1993,
Teddy Kollek was mayor of
Jerusalem, and it is due mostly to his
efforts and the unremitting work of
his colleagues that Jerusalem became
and has remained an open and
pluralistic city. Its multicultural
elements create a mosaic integrating
the numerous groups of its
heterogeneous population, and the
ugly marks of the city's division
have almost disappeared. Jerusalem
cannot be divided again; only after
its reunification did it begin truly to
live out its destiny. Neither can the
city be internationalized—this
solution, proposed by the United
Nations in 1947, proved unaccept-
able to both Muslims and Jews.

The world community fervently
hopes that Jews and Arabs will
continue to search for and find an
accommodation that is acceptable to
all sides so that the message of peace
may continue to emanate from
Jerusalem.

and the Israeli people set out to
rebuild the city. The Knesset, the
Israeli parliament, was established in
West Jerusalem, and other
government buildings, the Hebrew
University, new residential
neighborhoods, parks, and gardens
turned the Israeli part of Jerusalem
into a lively city and a modern
capital.

By contrast, development in East
Jerusalem stagnated under Jordanian
rule, and this part of the city
remained neglected. In the heart of
Jerusalem, the Old City, neglect and
decay were particularly marked and
little care was taken of the many
historic monuments and holy sites.
Fifty-eight synagogues and many
other buildings in the Jewish Quarter
were blown up to eradicate all
memory of Jewish presence in the
Old City.

Under Jordanian rule, East
Jerusalem did not become an Arab
capital—Jordan's capital was
Amman—and apart from being one
of Islam's holy cities, Jerusalem did
not seem greatly to interest the king
of Jordan.

Jerusalem remained divided for
nineteen years. Concrete walls and
barbed wire separated its two parts,
and Arab snipers shot at passersby
on the Jewish side. Article 8 of the
armistice agreement, which guar-
anteed free access on the Jordanian
side to the holy sites of all three
religions, was not respected by
Jordan. Foreigners were allowed to
cross into the Jordanian side of the
city via the only existing checkpoint,
the famous "Mandelbaum Gate," but
were not permitted to return into
West Jerusalem.

Jerusalem reunited

In 1967 continuing tension between
Israel and the surrounding Arab
states led to an alliance between
Jordan, Syria, and Egypt, whose
armies simultaneously attacked
Israel. The ensuing Six-Day War
brought East Jerusalem and the Old
City into Israeli hands. When they
took the Old City, Israeli troops were
particularly careful not to damage
the holy sites. The Temple Mount
and the Western Wall, as well as
Muslim mosques and Christian

3

The Old City—and Beyond

"Jerusalem is builded as a city that is compact together."
(Psalm 122:3)

An Old City street.

Opposite: A characteristic rooftop view of the Old City.

Walls and gates

Right: A shopping street in the Old City, viewed from the Damascus Gate.

When we talk of Jerusalem, we tend to envisage the Old City—the small area of some 220 acres (one square kilometer) bounded by the impressive walls constructed by the Ottoman Turks in the sixteenth century. These walls contain a huge variety of sacred sites—Christian, Jewish, and Islamic—the whole area being heavily built-up and crisscrossed with a maze of narrow, bustling, and confusing streets. Dominating the entire Old City is the vast *Haram Al Sharif*, or Noble Sanctuary, today the site of the Islamic Dome of the Rock and Aqsa Mosque, and in former times the site of the Jewish Temple. Within the Old City, and in a confusing mixture, can be found the remains of fortifications dating from Old Testament times; Hasmonean remains; Herodian towers and ruins; Roman arches and columns; Byzantine churches and streets; sites revered for centuries by Christians as associated with the life of Christ; early Christian sanctuaries; Arab shrines; Crusader relics; and Mameluk structures.

The walls
The present walls were rebuilt on the line of earlier fortifications by Suleiman the Magnificent in 1537-41. They measure over 4000 meters (4400 yards) in circumference and are continuous, with seven gates in use today for entering and leaving the city. The defensive walls are, of course, quite incapable of withstanding modern military assault; yet they retain a symbolic purpose, defining and containing the Old City. One steps into a different, older, and more memorable world as one enters the city gates. The narrow, crooked streets, the rich mix of architectural styles, the thronging pedestrians are redolent of a medieval walled town.

The city gates
There is little vehicular traffic through the city; the only places where motor traffic can enter are where the walls have been specially breached—at the Jaffa Gate, Dung Gate, and St. Stephen's Gate.

The Damascus Gate was built by the Turks on the site of an earlier Roman gate. Its Arabic name means "Gate of the Column"; the Romans

erected a column just inside the gate to honor the emperors Hadrian and Antoninus Pius. The Crusaders knew it as St. Stephen's Gate, as they believed it was outside this gate that the first Christian martyr was stoned to death; however, today another gate bears his name.

The Damascus Gate leads into the Muslim Quarter of the city and tends to be the busiest entrance. It is close to the East Jerusalem bus station and to the Arab district of East Jerusalem, and many Arabs use this gate to reach the markets inside the city.

In a clockwise direction around the walls, the next gate encountered is Herod's Gate, a smaller entrance with a direct passage rather than the

angled entry of the Damascus Gate (which was so designed for defensive purposes). Between the two gates are Solomon's Quarries, consisting of a huge, cavelike quarry which has been linked with the building exploits of King Solomon, Herod the Great, and Herod Agrippa.

Next is St. Stephen's Gate, which has had a confusing succession of names: The Arabs know it as St. Mary's Gate, since it leads to the tomb of Mary; the Crusaders knew it as the Gate of Jehoshaphat; and the Hebrew name is the Lions' Gate, since lions or heraldic panthers are found carved on its stonework. Like the Damascus Gate, the present

structure dates from the rebuilding of Suleiman the Magnificent in 1538.

The Golden Gate

The next gate encountered, traveling in the same direction, is the Golden Gate, which is now blocked. This may have been the site of the Herodian gate through which, in the days when the Temple still stood, the scapegoat was driven on the Day of Atonement, symbolically representing the goat's carrying away the sins of the people. During the Crusader period, the Golden Gate was opened just twice a year: for a solemn procession on Palm Sunday and for the Feast of the Exaltation of the Cross. But since that period, the gate has been blocked.

The Golden Gate has many traditions attaching to it, probably because it opens directly onto the Temple Mount area, once the site of Herod's Temple and now the site of the Dome of the Rock. Both Jews and Muslims believe that on the Day of Judgment the righteous will pass through this gate; and many Christians believe that Jesus entered this gate on the first Palm Sunday and that he will enter Jerusalem by the same gate at his Second Coming.

The Dung Gate, the closest gate to the Western Wall was also built in the sixteenth century but enlarged by the Jordanians when the Jaffa Gate was closed to traffic in 1948.

The Zion Gate on Mount Zion is also known by the Arabs as the Gate

of the Prophet David. It was badly damaged in the war of 1948. As in the case of other gates and of the Ottoman walls themselves, careful conservation has now been put in hand.

The Jaffa Gate
Next we come to the Jaffa Gate, known to the Crusaders as the Gate of David, and which still looks much as it did when first built by Suleiman the Magnificent. Although the original gate is still in use by pedestrians entering the city, the wall immediately alongside the gate was breached in 1898 to allow the German kaiser Wilhelm II to enter the Old City riding in his carriage. By contrast, the British general Allenby, approaching the city as conqueror in 1917, dismounted his horse and entered the city on foot, as pilgrims have done throughout history. The Jaffa Gate has a stone inscription in Arabic dedicating it to Suleiman.

The last gate on this tour is the New Gate, built in 1887 by the Ottoman Turks and leading to the Christian Quarter of the city.

The Temple Mount
Possibly the largest and almost certainly the most revered religious enclosure in the world, this area is holy to all three great monotheistic religions—Jews, Muslims, and Christians. The whole area, known in Arabic as the *Haram al-Sharif* (Noble Sanctuary) and in Hebrew as *Har ha-Moriyya* (Mount Moriah) and as the Temple Mount and Holy House, is the focal point of the city. It is situated on a raised platform occupying about fourteen hectares (thirty-four acres), which amounts to almost one-sixth of the entire area of the Old City.

The Temple Mount is dominated today by the unmistakable structure known as the Dome of the Rock and by the great Aqsa Mosque. These two Islamic buildings stand in magnificent solitude on the brilliant stone platform with its unrivaled views across to the Mount of Olives. The remainder of the platform is in places occupied by the welcome foliage of trees and shrubs, offering shade from the sun to the many pilgrims and tourists, and by a number of much smaller structures and dividing walls.

Above: An Arab grocer's stall in the Old City.

Left: Tourists in the Old City.

Opposite: The crowded bazaar in the Old City.

Right: Clothing shops in the Old City.

Mount Moriah

The Muslims revere this place as the site of the rock on Mount Moriah where Abraham attempted to sacrifice his son Isaac in obedience to God, but was prevented from doing so by an angel (Genesis 22), God providing a ram for Abraham to sacrifice in place of his son. The rock believed to mark the place of sacrifice is today covered by the golden hemisphere of the Dome of the Rock.

But the rock was of recurring importance in the early history of the city. When King David captured the city 3000 years ago, he disobeyed God by taking a census of his people. As punishment for his sin, the nation was visited by plague, though Jerusalem itself won an eleventh-hour reprieve when the Angel of Death, sword bared, stood on the great rock which overlooked the city (then sited on Mount Ophel, to the south of this site). To commemorate this event, David purchased the rock from its previous owner, Araunah (Ornan) the Jebusite, who had used it as a threshing floor and built an altar there, where he sacrificed in repentance (2 Samuel 24:18-25).

Although King David had wanted to build a temple in Jerusalem, he was forbidden to do so because he was a soldier whose hands were bloody from many campaigns. It was left to his son Solomon to fulfill David's ambition and build the first Temple on this site. Solomon started construction of the Temple in the fourth year of his reign, about 961 B.C., and finished in the eleventh year

Below: A cobbler at work on a city street.

Opposite: A fruiterer and confectioner in the Old City.

Right: A veiled Arab woman passes an ancient arch in the Old City.

Preparing to build

At that time when David saw that the LORD *had answered him in the threshing floor of Ornan the Jebusite, then he sacrificed there. For the tabernacle of the* LORD, *which Moses made in the wilderness, and the altar of the burnt offering, were at that season in the high place at Gibeon. But David could not go before it to inquire of God: for he was afraid because of the sword of the angel of the* LORD.

Then David said, This is the house of the LORD *God, and this is the altar of the burnt offering for Israel. And David commanded to gather together the strangers that were in the land of Israel; and he set masons to hew wrought stones to build the house of God. And David prepared iron in abundance for the nails for the doors of the gates, and for the joinings; and brass in abundance without weight; also cedar trees in abundance: for the Zidonians and they of Tyre brought much cedar wood to David. And David said, Solomon my son is young and tender, and the house that is to be builded for the* LORD *must be exceeding magnificent, of fame and of glory throughout all countries: I will therefore now make preparation for it. So David prepared abundantly before his death.*

1 Chronicles 21:28–22:5

(1 Kings 6:37,38). He was aided in the work by King Hiram of Tyre, who supplied both men and materials, including the famed cedars of Lebanon. Solomon's Temple was constructed in stone and timber, and the interior richly decorated with gold and with cedar wood. The building faced east and, like the portable Tabernacle used by the Israelites during their years of wandering in the wilderness and which it replaced, had a large altar in front for animal sacrifices.

Shortly after its completion the Temple was looted by the Egyptian Pharaoh Shishak, in about 923 B.C. (1 Kings 14:25,26). Centuries later it was completely destroyed by the

invading Babylonians in 587 B.C., who carried the Israelites into captivity.

When the Jews returned from exile between 536 and 515 B.C., the Israelite leader Zerubbabel oversaw the rebuilding of the Temple on the same site and probably in much the same style as the original. Although the sacrifices and rituals were now resumed much as they had been before the exile, the Ark of the Covenant no longer rested in the holiest place; it had been lost at the Babylonian invasion.

Herod's Temple

Antiochus IV of Syria sacked the Temple in 169 B.C. (1 Maccabees 1:20-

4). The Jewish people, led by the Maccabee family, resisted the invader. When the Maccabeans repulsed Antiochus, the Temple was both ritually cleansed and largely rebuilt.

We know little of Zerubbabel's Temple; by contrast, Herod's Temple, which replaced it, is comparatively well known to us. Archaeological discoveries, together with manuscript evidence from the *Mishnah* and from the Jewish historian Josephus, have combined to give us a quite full description of this magnificent structure.

Herod the Great commenced work on the Temple around 20 B.C., as part of his massive program of

Left: Street scene in the Old City.

Below: A fountain in the Arab market (*souk*) of the Old City.

Opposite right: The Dome of the Rock from the Old City, with the Mount of Olives in the background.

Below: The Dome of the Rock from the Mount of Olives in springtime.

ostentatious public works, which included his palace at Herodion, his palace at Masada and the port of Caesarea Maritima. We gain some direct evidence of the splendor of his building from the Western Wall itself, the lower courses of which date from his time.

Herod surrounded the crest of the hill with great retaining walls to build a vast platform—strong enough to have survived more or less intact. The lower parts of the platform masonry, differentiated by the characteristic finish of the Herodian stonemasons, witness to the high quality of the work.

The Temple enclosure had at its center the Temple sanctuary building, surrounded by a number of concentric courts, successively for Gentiles, Jewish women, Jewish men, and priests. Non-Jews were prohibited from entering further than the Court of the Gentiles, on pain of death. They were kept out by the wall of partition mentioned by the apostle Paul in Ephesians 2:14.

The Temple itself again faced east, and was in plan similar to Solomon's Temple, though much more lavish in its use of materials. Part of the building was covered with gold plate; the remainder was finished in white marble. Inside the Temple, as in Solomon's Temple, stood the symbolic furniture, consisting of the altar of incense, the table of shew-bread, and the golden candlestick. In front of the Temple stood the great square altar of sacrifice, where King Herod sacrificed 300 oxen to celebrate the completion of the building.

This building, fully described by the Jewish historian Flavius Josephus, was the Temple known so well by Jesus of Nazareth, and which

is mentioned so frequently in the Gospels. It was here that Jesus was found debating with the Jewish teachers on his first visit to Jerusalem with his parents. It was here, too, that he overturned the money-changers' tables.

Destruction

However, Herod's Temple remained standing for a very brief period. During the First Jewish Revolt of 66-73 A.D., the Romans completely destroyed the building, as Josephus describes graphically in his *Jewish War*. For many years the area remained in ruins. It is unclear what, if anything, was constructed on the Temple Mount when the Romans rebuilt the city of Aelia Capitolina on the site, and for at least a century Jews were completely banned from the city.

Not until the Arab conquest of Jerusalem in 638 and the rise of Islam did the area become of major significance again, since for Christians the sites connected with Jesus' death and burial were of much more significance. The Muslims immediately started to build the Aqsa Mosque around 639, while the

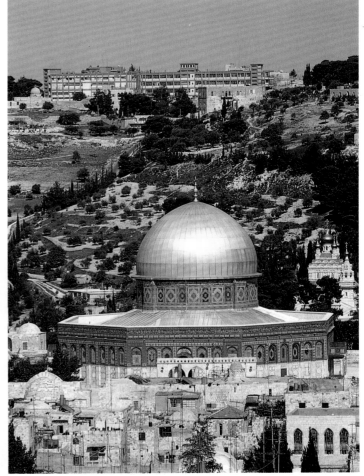

Solomon's Temple

And it came to pass in the four hundred and eightieth year after the children of Israel were come out of the land of Egypt, in the fourth year of Solomon's reign over Israel . . . that he began to build the house of the LORD. And the house which king Solomon built for the LORD, the length thereof was threescore cubits, and the breadth thereof twenty cubits, and the height thereof thirty cubits. And the porch before the temple of the house, twenty cubits was the length thereof, according to the breadth of the house; and ten cubits was the breadth thereof before the house. And for the house he made windows of narrow lights. . . .

And the house, when it was in building, was built of stone made ready before it was brought thither: so that there was neither hammer nor axe nor any tool of iron heard in the house, while it was in building. . . . So he built the house, and finished it; and covered the house with beams and boards of cedar.

1 Kings 6:1-9

Opposite: The Dome of
the Winds, or Spirits
(*Qubbat al Arwah*).

The Temple Mount

Right: The *Haram al-
Sharif*, is dominated by
the Dome of the Rock.

Below: The ablutions
fountain, *al-Kas*, and
Dome of the Rock.

Dome of the Rock (begun in 688 and
finished in 691) is the only early
major Islamic sanctuary to have
survived more or less as it was built.

The furthermost place
For Muslims the site is important not
only because of Abraham's
attempted sacrifice of Isaac, but also
because it is believed that the
Prophet Muhammad was carried off
by the archangel Gabriel on a
winged horse to the "furthermost
place" (*el aqsa*), from which he rose
to heaven. In heaven Muhammad is
said to have met God face to face,
returning home the same night
bearing with him God's commandments for his followers. For this
reason the *"El Aqsa"* mosque became
a particularly sacred site for Islam.
The builder, Abd al-Malik, also had
his own ambitions; he wished to
impress his fellow Arabs by showing
that Muslims could build

Below: Part of the Western Wall tunnels, dug beneath the Temple Mount, which have revealed the entire length of the Western Wall – almost 448 meters.

magnificent structures to rival the Christian shrines of Jerusalem.

The Dome of the Rock

Often in the past wrongly known as the Mosque of Omar, the Dome of the Rock is one of the finest—and most ancient—buildings of Islam. It gleams both inside and out with rich golds, turquoises, and other colors, and has often been compared with a perfect gemstone. The Dome is the third holiest place in the Islamic world, after the *Ka'aba* in Mecca and the Prophet's Mosque in Medina, and many Muslims visit it as part of the great annual pilgrimage to the holy places of Mecca and Jerusalem.

The Dome is not a mosque, and was not designed to hold a large congregation; it was constructed to cover the Rock, and to provide a place of prayer and a focus for pilgrim visits. In accordance with the Muslim prohibition on depicting human forms, the surfaces of the Dome of the Rock are covered with elaborate floral and geometric decorations, as well as with fine Arabic calligraphy. The design of the Dome is in the Syrian-Byzantine tradition, and it was constructed by local workers and craftsmen.

At the center of the Dome is the

The Temple rebuilt

And the elders of the Jews builded, and they prospered through the prophesying of Haggai the prophet and Zechariah the son of Iddo. And they builded, and finished it, according to the commandment of the God of Israel, and according to the commandment of Cyrus, and Darius, and Artaxerxes king of Persia. And this house was finished on the third day of the month Adar, which was in the sixth year of the reign of Darius the king.

And the children of Israel, the priests, and the Levites, and the rest of the children of the captivity, kept the dedication of this house of God with joy.

Ezra 6:14-16

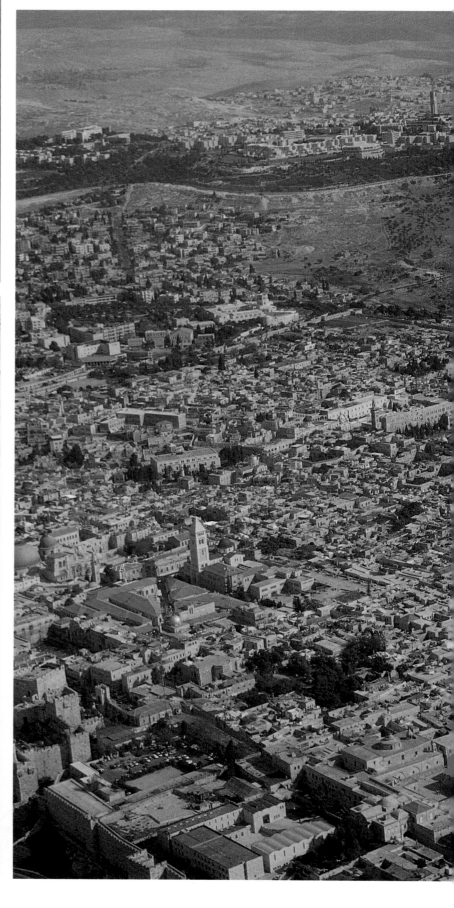

Holy Rock itself, surrounded by a wooden screen erected in 1199. A mark on the rock is venerated by Muslims as the footmark of the prophet Muhammad; the Crusaders believed they could discern the footprint of Christ on the same rock.

When the Crusaders conquered Jerusalem, they converted the building into a church, renaming it the Temple of the Lord. But after Saladin's recapture of the city in 1187, the building was quickly stripped of all Christian additions, such as the altar, and restored to its original purpose as an Islamic holy place. Since that time there have been numerous additions, alterations, and repairs to the building, which nevertheless retains essentially its original appearance.

The Aqsa Mosque

By contrast with the Dome, the Aqsa Mosque is a true congregational mosque, the largest in Jerusalem, and on Fridays it is thronged with praying Muslims. Its precise origins are unclear, though it is of early Islamic construction and was for a short time used by the Crusaders as a palace. Although the Aqsa Mosque has been very extensively restored, especially after several severe earthquakes and a disastrous fire in 1969, the building has essentially evolved from the original seventh- or eighth-century structure. There is a tradition that the murderers of the medieval Archbishop of Canterbury, Thomas Becket, were buried here.

Below: Aerial view of the Old City of Jerusalem, showing clearly the area occupied by the *Haram al-Sharif*, or Noble Sanctuary. In the middle distance can be seen the Garden of Gethsemane and Mount of Olives; in the distance, the Judean Hills.

Tunnels

In 1967, after the Six-Day War, the Israeli authorities set about attempting to expose some of the hidden parts of the wall surrounding the Temple Mount. This entailed extensive tunneling operations, as a result of which the entire length of the Western Wall of the Temple Mount was revealed—nearly 448 meters (500 yards) in all. In addition, a number of rooms and public halls were discovered, as well as a section of road dating from the Second Temple period, and a pool. All these may now be visited as part of the Western Wall Tunnels, administered by the Ministry of Religious Affairs.

The *Via Dolorosa*

Christians recognize a traditional route by which they believe Jesus was led from judgment before Pontius Pilate to the cross at Golgotha, marking seven—or fourteen, according to a different tradition—places, or "Stations," where particular events occurred on the way. Each Station is marked by a special plaque. The route begins at the so-called *Ecce Homo* arch (meaning "This is the man"), thus named because it is believed that here, on an ancient pavement of smooth stones, was the place where Pilate sat in judgment over Jesus (John 19:1-3). (It is now regarded as

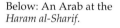

Below: An Arab at the *Haram al-Sharif*.

unlikely that this is the correct site; Pontius Pilate was probably in residence at the Citadel on the west of the city when he sat in judgment on Jesus.) The first and second Stations are sited at the Chapel of the Flagellation. The third Station, marked by a Polish Catholic chapel, marks the place where Jesus is believed to have stumbled, and the fourth, nearby, the point where Jesus met his mother, Mary.

The Stations proceed through neighboring narrow streets in this way, with the final Stations being situated inside the Church of the Holy Sepulchre, which both tradition and scholarship hold to be the

authentic site of Jesus' crucifixion and entombment.

The Church of the Holy Sepulchre

Although this is in a sense the central church of the Christian world, many visitors find it a terrible disappointment. It in no way compares in either magnificence or solemnity with the great buildings of St. Peter's, Rome, or St. Sophia, Istanbul. It is surprisingly difficult to find, being surrounded by closely crowded (and for the most part undistinguished) buildings. Inside, it is rather dark and invariably crowded, and more often than not noisy with tourists and competing services. Six different

Above: *El Kas*, the ritual washing-place on the Haram Platform, or Temple Mount area.

Purifying the Temple

Then said Judas and his brethren, Behold, our enemies are discomfited: let us go up to cleanse the sanctuary. Upon this all the host assembled themselves together, and went up into mount Sion. . . . Then they took whole stones according to the law, and built a new altar according to the former; and made up the sanctuary, and the things that were within the temple, and hallowed the courts. . . . And upon the altar they burned incense, and the lamps that were upon the candlestick they lighted that they might give light in the temple.

1 Maccabees 4:36,37,47,48,50

Right: The entrance to the Aqsa Mosque, *Haram al-Sharif.*

Christian traditions claim an interest in the building—Roman Catholics, Greek Orthodox, Armenians, Syrians, Copts, and Ethiopians.

As mentioned earlier, it does seem very likely that the church is built over the true site of Jesus' death and burial. We know that Jesus was crucified at Golgotha, the place of the skull—that is, a rocky mound which resembled a skull (John 19:17), and that a tomb lay close by (John 19: 41,42). In the first century A.D., at the time of Jesus' earthly ministry, the site was a disused stone quarry and was located outside the city walls. Tombs, possibly dating from the first century, have been found cut into the quarry walls.

But the evidence is stronger than this. As early as 66 A.D. the Jerusalem believers are known to have observed religious celebrations on this site, and it must be significant that the site remained unbuilt on even when it was taken within the city walls in 41-43 A.D. Moreover, when the Emperor Constantine decided to build a church on the site of the resurrection, he clearly paid attention to local knowledge and chose this site—even though it entailed the additional cost and effort of demolishing a temple of Venus which had been constructed meantime on the site by one of his predecessors, the Emperor Hadrian. He would surely not have gone to this trouble and expense without very good reason indeed.

During the excavations for Constantine's new church, Bishop Makarios of Jerusalem discovered a rock-cut tomb on the site, as well as the hillock believed to be Golgotha, and a Roman cistern into which several execution crosses had been thrown. Constantine's empress, Helena, claimed that one of these was Jesus' cross, the "True Cross," and it soon became an important relic of the church.

Eusebius, the early Christian historian and bishop of Caesarea,

witnessed these excavations and reported that "as layer after layer of soil was revealed, the venerable and holiest memorial of our Saviour's resurrection came into view. . . ."

Following these excavations, the site was leveled, but the rock of Golgotha and the tomb were left so that the church could be constructed over them.

Constantine's church

Work began on Constantine's church in 326, and the building was dedicated in 335. It incorporated an open courtyard surrounding the place believed to be Golgotha, with the True Cross above it, and a circular structure built around the supposed tomb of Jesus, as well as a large, five-aisled basilica.

Although set on fire by the Persians in 614, the church was reconstructed along its original lines in 629 by the Abbot Modestus, and the True Cross, retrieved from the Persians, was re-erected in Golgotha. But in 1009 the Muslim caliph El Hakim systematically vandalized the church, almost completely destroying it. The church, desperately short of money, was unable to repair the entire building. As a result, a large part of the church was lost for all time, and only the circular rotunda and courtyard remained when the

Byzantine Emperor Constantine IX Monomachos rebuilt the church in 1048.

The Crusaders took possession of the church on capturing Jerusalem in 1099 and remodeled it, completing their work in 1149. They covered the courtyard with a Romanesque church, and later added a belltower. Thus today the church retains its two vital features—the rotunda surrounding the tomb, and the (now covered) courtyard around Golgotha. When the Muslim leader Saladin retook the city in 1187, he agreed not to destroy the church, but removed the cross, destroyed the bells, and locked the doors.

Opposite: The Bethesda Pools, part of which is said to date from the eighth century B.C. This was the site of Jesus' miracle of healing the crippled man (John 5:1-13).

Healing at Bethesda

In these lay a great multitude of impotent folk, of blind, halt, withered, waiting for the moving of the water. For an angel went down at a certain season into the pool, and troubled the water: whosoever then first after the troubling of the water stepped in was made whole of whatsoever disease he had. And a certain man was there, which had an infirmity thirty and eight years. When Jesus saw him lie, and knew that he had been now a long time in that case, he saith unto him, Wilt thou be made whole? The impotent man answered him, Sir, I have no man, when the water is troubled, to put me into the pool: but while I am coming, another steppeth down before me. Jesus saith unto him, Rise, take up thy bed, and walk. And immediately the man was made whole, and took up his bed, and walked: and on the same day was the sabbath.

The Jews therefore said unto him that was cured, It is the sabbath day: it is not lawful for thee to carry thy bed. He answered them, He that made me whole, the same said unto me, Take up thy bed, and walk. Then asked they him, What man is that which said unto thee, Take up thy bed, and walk? And he that was healed wist not who it was: for Jesus had conveyed himself away, a multitude being in that place.

John 5:3-13

NE CORNER OF THE
SOUTHERN POOL.
ANGLE NORD-EST
DU BASSIN SUD.

Right: A Coptic nun.

Although in the first years after Saladin's victory Christians were barred from the city, these restrictions were gradually lifted, until by the fourteenth century Latin, Greek, Georgian, Armenian, Jacobite, Coptic, and Ethiopian Christians all had right of access to the building. Wisely, in view of the many disputes before and since, the main door keys were retained by Muslims—for centuries by one family, the Nuseibeh family.

There followed further destruction and desecration, including a fire in 1808 and an earthquake in 1927. In 1834 it is estimated that 300 pilgrims were crushed to death during an Easter service when panic spread through the overcrowded building as a result of excessive smoke from candles.

Ownership of the church is still shared by six different religious communities. The Roman Catholic church (or Latins) owns the southern part of the rock of Golgotha, part of the choir of the church, the Epiphany Chapel, the Mary Magdalene Altar, and the Chapel of the Finding of the Cross; the Greek Orthodox Church owns the nave, the northern part of Golgotha, the Chapel of Adam beneath it, and "Christ's prison"; to the Armenians belong the Place of the Three Marys, the east chapel in the ambulatory, and the chapel of St. Helena; the Coptic Christians have the chapel behind the Holy Tomb;

Below: Orthodox Christians with candles.

The Light of Life

Then spake Jesus again unto them, saying, I am the light of the world: he that followeth me shall not walk in darkness, but shall have the light of life. The Pharisees therefore said unto him, Thou bearest record of thyself; thy record is not true. Jesus answered and said unto them, Though I bear record of myself, yet my record is true: for I know whence I came, and whither I go; but ye cannot tell whence I come, and whither I go.

John 8:12-14

Above: A Greek Orthodox priest in the Old City.

Left: An Orthodox pilgrim lights a lantern.

the Syrians the west chapel in the rotunda; and the Abyssinians, or Ethiopians, the Tomb of Joseph of Arimathea.

By the early twentieth century the church had fallen into serious decay. At last in 1959 the Latin, Greek, and Armenian churches agreed to a program of major structural repairs, which included the removal of many of the partitions and other additions made over the centuries and the restoration of the building to something approximating its twelfth-century appearance.

The final Stations

As mentioned previously, the final Stations of the cross are found within the church itself. The tenth and eleventh Stations, marking the places where Jesus is believed to have been disrobed and nailed to the cross, are both found at the top of a steep staircase at Golgotha, or Calvary. Two chapels are built on the rock; one is known as the Altar of the Crucifixion, the other as the Chapel of Sorrows. The twelfth Station, in the Chapel of the Exaltation (or Raising) of the Cross, consists of a rock with a slot cut to accommodate the cross. The thirteenth Station, the Stabat Mater, marks the place where Mary is held to have received the body after it had been taken down from the cross.

The site of Jesus' tomb and resurrection is now marked by an early nineteenth-century marble chapel. The original tomb, revealed by Constantine in the fourth century, was destroyed by al-Hakim in 1009. The little Chapel of the Holy Sepulchre, reached by a low door, is the fourteenth and final Station of the Cross. The chapel itself is an elaborate Turkish rococo-style structure with forty-three lamps hanging over the entrance—thirteen each for the Armenian, Latin, and Greek churches, and four for the Coptic church. Clustered on the roof of the Crypt of St. Helena, part of the Church of the Holy Sepulchre, is a cluster of mud huts belonging to the Ethiopian Christians and forming a *laura*, or Orthodox monastery. It is possible for the visitor to walk through the monastery and to sample the flavor of the distinctive and colorful Ethiopian art. The Ethiopians inhabit the ruins of a medieval cloister built by the Crusaders; their quiet religious dignity contrasts powerfully with the noisy and tiring bustle in the main parts of the church. The Ethiopian Christians apparently celebrate Christmas every month.

The churches of Jerusalem

Jerusalem has a special place in the hearts of Christian believers. Names such as the Mount of Olives, Garden of Gethsemane, the *Via Dolorosa*, and Golgotha vividly call to mind events described in the Gospels. Churches have been built on almost every site connected with the events of the Passion.

Within the Old City the visitor is confronted by a bewildering range of churches, chapels, and cathedrals. Almost every major church and denomination has staked its claim to a place in this holy city, which represents the focus of the Christian world. We cannot here mention all the churches, but attempt to discuss some of the more interesting.

The Church of St. Anne

The Church of St. Anne, built by the Crusaders near the Lion Gate (now known as St. Stephen's Gate), was named after the grandmother of Jesus. It was built on the site of a fifth-century Byzantine church built by Eudocia in honor of Mary. Although this church was destroyed in 614 by the Persians, it was rebuilt shortly afterwards. The Crusaders rededicated the church to St. Anne, and their church has been preserved in its original austere beauty—a style typical of the twelfth century. The church is probably the finest surviving example of Romanesque

Right: These stones are believed by archaeologists to be part of the original roadway over which Jesus passed on his way to the crucifixion.

Calvary

And as they led [Jesus] away, they laid hold upon one Simon, a Cyrenian, coming out of the country, and on him they laid the cross, that he might bear it after Jesus. . . .

And when they were come to the place, which is called Calvary, there they crucified him, and the malefactors, one on the right hand, and the other on the left.

Luke 23:26,33

Opposite: The traditional *Via Dolorosa*, along which it is said Jesus passed on his way to his crucifixion.

Right: A street scene in the Old City.

architecture in Jerusalem.

In 1187 after the Crusaders had been defeated at the Battle of Hattin, the Muslim leader Saladin converted this church into a Medress *Qu'ran* school, and it remained in Arab hands for 700 years. In the nineteenth century the Turkish sultan handed the church over to the French in thanks for their military assistance during the Crimean War. However, by that time it was in a sorry state; the Turks believed it was haunted, and the Turkish governor had stabled his horses there. Rubbish deposited inside the church reached almost to the roof.

A careful examination of the facade of the church reveals that it is slightly tilted, a type of construction common in medieval France and intended to symbolize the body of the crucified Jesus. The interior is in Burgundian Romanesque style, with strong, simple pillars supporting a vaulted nave. A new high altar was carved by the French sculptor Philippe Kaeppelin in 1954 and shows the Annunciation, the birth of Christ, and his deposition from the cross.

The Pool of Bethesda

Next to the Church of St. Anne lies the Pool of Bethesda, believed by Christians to be the place where Jesus performed the miracle described in John 5. We know that the Romans were well aware of the healing powers of the pool for the sick, blind, and lame. The north pool is believed to date from a much earlier period, around the eighth

Below: The seventh Station of the Cross on the traditional *Via Dolorosa*, or Way of the Cross.

Opposite: The traditional site of Jesus' grave, in the Church of the Holy Sepulchre.

Right: The Church of the Holy Sepulchre, traditional site of Jesus' burial.

century B.C., when it supplied the first Temple with water. Archaeological excavations have confirmed the biblical description of the pool and have revealed remains from various successive periods of the pool.

The pool consists of two basins, probably constructed in the Maccabean period. Archaeologists have discovered earthenware and coins here dating from the Hasmonean period (second century B.C.–63 A.D.), which includes the time

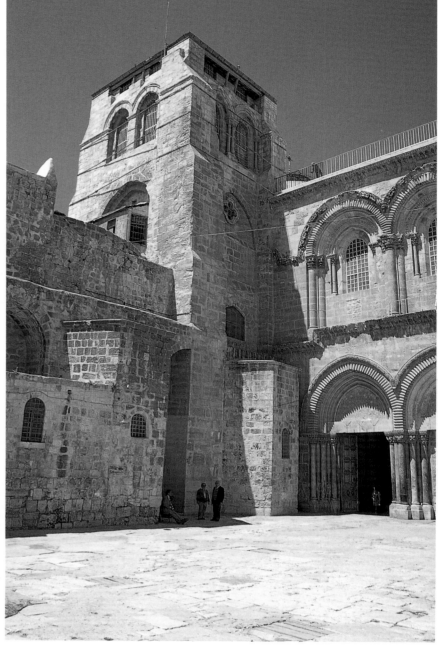

Above: The twelfth Station of the Cross, the Raising of the Cross, inside the Church of the Holy Sepulchre.

Right: The complex roofs of the Church of the Holy Sepulchre.

Opposite: The ornate
entrance to the traditional
site of Jesus' burial, in the
Church of the Holy
Sepulchre, Jerusalem.

Right: The interior of the
Church of the Holy
Sepulchre during a
service.

Opposite: Pilgrims carry a cross during the Good Friday processions in Jerusalem.

Right: Orthodox priests.

of Christ. By the second century A.D. a shrine to the god Asclepius, deity of healing, had been established here, and in the nineteenth century a number of votive offerings to this god were found here. The Byzantines built a basilica on this site in the fifth century, but this was destroyed in the eleventh century.

The Church of Mary Magdalene
There is a very early tradition that the place now known as the Garden of Gethsemane (just outside the Old City) is where Jesus prayed in agony and where Judas Iscariot came with armed guards to betray his master (Matthew 26:36-56). Early Christian pilgrims write of visiting the site,

and by 384 A.D. a church had been erected here, incorporating a rock on which, by tradition, Jesus prayed in preparation for the ordeal to come.

The most impressive of all the churches in Gethsemane is the Church of Mary Magdalene, a building boasting seven onion-shaped cupolas. Built by Czar

Alexander III in 1888 in memory of his mother, Maria Alexandrovna, a princess of Hesse, it is typical of seventeenth-century Russian architecture. Flood-lit at night, it has the appearance of a fantastic wedding cake. Diagonal cross beams attached to the crosses protruding from the domes symbolize the resurrection. The Russian artists Vereshaguine and Ivanov were responsible for the interior decorations.

The tomb of Grandduchess Elizabeth Feodorovna, the czar's sister assassinated in 1918, is in the crypt of this church. Elizabeth and her husband, Duke Sergei of Moscow, helped found the Imperial Orthodox Society of Palestine. After the duchess was killed during the 1917 Russian Revolution, her body was brought to Jerusalem via Peking in fulfillment of her request to be buried in this church.

The church, together with the adjoining monastery, belongs to the White Russian Orthodox Church, which is based today in the United States of America. In the courtyard

Right: Ethiopian Christians at the Church of the Holy Sepulchre.

of the monastery can be seen the remains of some steps, possibly those described in a ninth-century manuscript which mentions the eastern approach to the city of Jerusalem, consisting of 537 steps down from the Mount of Olives into the Kidron Valley and a further 195 steps leading up from the valley to St. Stephen's Gate.

The Church of All Nations
Below the Russian church is found the Church of All Nations, the facade of which gleams out from between the dark green trees of the Garden of Gethsemane. In earlier times an oil press stood here, serving the nearby olive grove, as its Hebrew name *Gat Schemanium* (olive press) reminds us. It is said that some of the gnarled,

knotted trees in the garden are more than 2000 years old. It was here that Jesus often spent time with his disciples; and here, too, that he was arrested and led away by soldiers.

The site was first consecrated by Byzantine Christians, and remains of their fourth-century church are still visible. After that church was destroyed by an earthquake, a

second church was built in the twelfth century by the Crusaders but abandoned in 1345.

The site then remained desolate until 1919, when the present church was erected; its name reflects that it was built with money donated by all the nations of the world. A splendid mosaic over the facade portrays Jesus as the mediator between man and his Creator, the God to whom all nations look in hope. Above his head appear the Greek letters alpha and omega, illustrating the words of Revelation 1:8: "I am Alpha and Omega, the beginning and the ending, saith the Lord, which is, and which was, and which is to come, the Almighty." On the columns stand statues of the four evangelists Matthew, Mark, Luke, and John. The stags, standing opposite each other, remind us of David's words in the psalm: "As the hart panteth after the water brooks, so panteth my soul after thee, O God" (Psalm 42:12).

Dominus Flevit Chapel

A much more recent and more modest building is the Franciscan Dominus Flevit Chapel. It was built to commemorate the spot where tradition has it Jesus wept over the city of Jerusalem (Luke 19:41) and is built over the site of a fifth-century church. Very simple in design, it is intended to resemble the shape of a teardrop and incorporates a mosaic from the fifth-century church in its structure. This charming building affords a splendid view over the Old City, something of which many photographers have availed themselves.

Pater Noster Church

A little further up the slope of the Mount of Olives stands the Pater Noster Church, constructed over the site of the Eleona Basilica, or Church of the Disciples and Ascension, built by Emperor Constantine in 326-333. Constantine built his church over a cave from which it was believed Jesus ascended. Later, however, the site associated with the ascension shifted further up the hill.

Although the Persians destroyed the original building in 614, the Crusaders rebuilt on the same site. By now the location had come to be revered as the place where Jesus had taught his disciples the Lord's Prayer (the *"Pater Noster,"* in Latin). However, by the nineteenth century the church was in ruins; in 1851 the stones were sold as tombstones. In 1868 the French Princesse de la Tour d'Auvergne built a cloister on the site, later adding a Carmelite convent. Since her chapel was built to mark where Jesus taught his disciples the Lord's Prayer (Luke 11:2-4), the words of the prayer are

inscribed in sixty-eight different languages on colored tiles around the cloister.

The Chapel of the Ascension

This chapel is situated in the Arab village of et-Tur, and now falls within the precincts of a mosque.

It is from this place, on the summit of the Mount of Olives, that Jesus is believed to have ascended into heaven. Luke records in the Acts of the Apostles that the Ascension occurred forty days after Easter, on the Mount of Olives, a Sabbath's day journey out of the city—i.e. 2,000 paces.

The first church on this site was built before 392 by a Roman Christian lady, Poimenia. This structure was destroyed by the Persians in 614, rebuilt, and then reconstructed as an octagonal building by the Crusaders in 1102. However in 1198 Saladin gave the site to two of his followers, and it has been in Muslim hands ever since.

The chapel consists of an octagonal outer wall, which has hooks fastened to it from which Christians suspend

a temporary roof during the feast of the Ascension. Within the surrounding walls stands a shell-shaped cupola or edicule resting on four columns, giving the monument an air of weightless elegance. Beneath the dome of the chapel lies a stone with a footprint, supposed to be that of Jesus.

The Syrian Orthodox Church of St. Mark

The Syrian Orthodox Church is one of the oldest of the Christian denominations present in the Holy Land and claims direct descent from Abraham. This church is the center of the Syrian Orthodox community, who today still use the ancient Syriac language. The church forms part of a convent believed to have been built on the site of the "House of Mark," where, tradition has it, the Last Supper and Pentecost took place. It is also held that Mary was baptized in an earlier church on this site. The present church, probably recon-structed by the Crusaders in 1200, was built on the foundations of a previous building and is situated

between the Armenian and Jewish Quarters. It was given back to the Syrian or Jacobite church when the Western Christians left Jerusalem in 1187.

The Russian Orthodox Church

There is a special attraction to be found in the wide variety of Jerusalem's architectural styles. At the heart of the busy, modern city, and outside the walls of the Old City, one suddenly bumps into a nineteenth-century Russian cathedral whose ten cupola towers stand not in the snowy landscape of Russia but under Israel's sun-drenched skies. This church, built in 1860 by the Russian Orthodox Society of Palestine, stands on a parcel of land placed at the disposal of Russian pilgrims to Jerusalem. The complex also includes a hospital, living quarters, and a prison which is still in use today. The whole complex was surrounded by a great wall to protect residents from the brigands who threatened the city. The building, no longer used by the Orthodox Church, is today rented out to the Israeli authorities.

The Armenian Cathedral of St. James

Visitors to the Armenian district must first pass through a heavy iron gate with the inscription in Armenian: "This gate was built by the Patriarch Krikor in 1646." The marble drinking fountain in the courtyard was built at the turn of the nineteenth century and carries the inscription: "May all who drink at

Opposite: The Lutheran Church of the Redeemer, consecrated in 1898.

Above: Cloisters of the Lutheran Church of the Redeemer.

Left: Interior of the Syrian Church of St. Mark.

Opposite: Easter service in the Church of the Holy Sepulchre.

Left: Candles in the Church of the Holy Sepulchre.

Jerusalem the Golden

Jerusalem the golden,
with milk and honey blest;
Beneath thy contemplation
sink heart and voice oprest.
I know not, O I know not
what joys await us there;
What radiancy of glory,
what bliss beyond compare.

There is the throne of David;
and there from care released,
The shout of them that triumph,
the song of them that feast:
And they who with their Leader
have conquered in the fight,
For ever and for ever
are clothed in robes of white.

Bernard of Cluny,
translated by J.M. Neale

Above: Nun with a cat.

Above right: Orthodox priest.

Right: Orthodox priest.

Left: A Coptic priest.

this well remember the anonymous builder."

The Armenians come from the southern Caucasus, the region around Mount Ararat, which is today in Armenia. St. Gregory brought Christianity to this region in the third century and gave his name to the Armenian, or Gregorian, Church.

St. James' Cathedral is built on the traditional site of the execution of James, son of Zebedee, whose death was ordered by Herod Agrippa II (Acts 12:2). The church was originally built on this site by Gregorian Christians in the eleventh century but sold to the Armenian Christians later in the twelfth

Above: An Armenian priest.

Left: An Orthodox priest.

century. The majority of the 3500 Armenians living in Jerusalem today are Gregorian Christians, speaking their own language, which derives from Indo-Teutonic, and living an active cultural life which helps maintain their identity. Many Armenians work in the arts and crafts, specializing in pottery and jewelry; they even have their own printing press in the city.

In the treasure vault of the Armenian patriarch are kept priceless works of art. Their library, named after the Armenian oil magnate Gulbenkian, who donated a huge sum for its construction in 1929, contains the handwritten holy *Thoros* and other important and valuable manuscripts.

The Church of the Redeemer

This German Lutheran church is the most recent in the Old City, having been erected in 1898, but follows the outline of the eleventh-century church of St. Mary of the Latins, which was converted into a mosque by Saladin after 1187. A particular attraction for the visitor is the tall tower, which can be climbed and

Right: An Orthodox priest.

Below: A Syrian priest at St. Mark's Church, with the *Codex Syricus* Bible.

which affords splendid views over the entire city, particularly of the Church of the Holy Sepulchre. Adjacent to the church is a Lutheran hospice, which incorporates the cloister of the medieval hospice.

The Dormition

A particularly prominent church standing on Mount Zion is the Dormitio Sanctae Mariae Church, or Dormition of the Virgin Mary. It marks the traditional location where Mary is said to have died, and it was consecrated in 1908. Today the church is looked after by German Benedictine monks.

The Nea Church

There are, of course, many other churches in the city. Among recent archaeological discoveries has been the remains of the Nea, or New, Church of Justinian in the Jewish Quarter of the Old City. This church, dedicated to Mary, Mother of God, was built by the Emperor Justinian and completed in 543 A.D. The largest basilica known in Palestine, it was renowned for its size and splendor. Parts of the remains have been preserved beneath the Batei Mahse and can be visited.

Near the Jaffa Gate and just inside the Old City walls is the Anglican Christ Church with its hospice, opened in 1849 after a joint initiative by Prussia and Britain to set up an English/Prussian bishopric in the city; whilst outside the Old City in East Jerusalem is St. George's Anglican Cathedral, built in 1898, after the Anglo-Prussian agreement broke down.

Above: Ethiopian priests in their colorful vestments.

Left: An Armenian priest.

Above: An Orthodox
priest in the Old City.

4

The Western Wall

"Let the children of Zion be joyful in their King."
(Psalm 149:2b)

A *Barmitzvah* at the Western Wall.

The Western Wall

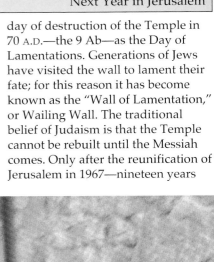
day of destruction of the Temple in 70 A.D.—the 9 Ab—as the Day of Lamentations. Generations of Jews have visited the wall to lament their fate; for this reason it has become known as the "Wall of Lamentation," or Wailing Wall. The traditional belief of Judaism is that the Temple cannot be rebuilt until the Messiah comes. Only after the reunification of Jerusalem in 1967—nineteen years

Right: Orthodox Jews in the Old City.

Since the beginning of the Diaspora (dispersion of the Jews), the Western Wall, or Wall of Lamentation, has formed a link between dispersed Jews and the rest of the world following the destruction of the Temple by the Roman emperor Titus in 70 A.D. For centuries it was believed that the wall was the only part of the magnificent Herodian Temple to survive Titus' destruction. Because for many centuries the city authorities prohibited the Jews from setting foot on the holy mountain, Mount Moriah, the wall came to symbolize for them the Temple itself. In the course of time it became a sacred monument in its own right.

Two thousand years later this wall has become a memorial for the Jews, reminding them of their times of loss and captivity. That loss was so tragic that the Jewish calendar marks the

Below: An elderly Orthodox Jew.

after the founding of the modern State of Israel—did the Jews once more take possession of the Western Wall. The sight of hundreds of exhausted Israeli soldiers crying at the wall, having entered this holy site for the first time after years of exclusion, will never be erased from the memory of those who were present that day. Since that historic event, thousands of Jews from all over the world have come to pray unhindered at the wall.

The area is today divided into separate men's and women's enclosures, as Orthodox Jewish law requires, and is particularly busy on Sabbath and festival days. Orthodox Jews will not enter the *Haram al Sharif* itself, fearing they might in error stand over the site of the holiest place, and thus transgress Jewish law. During the last ten years, intensive archaeological research has revealed much more about the Temple, confirming how impressive this building must have appeared in Herodian times. Nevertheless the Wall of Lamentations remains the emotional heart of this historic site.

The very stones of the wall reveal much about the history of Jerusalem. The top seven layers of the wall,

Right: Jewish schoolboys
at the Western Wall.

Right: A boy reads from
the Jewish Scriptures on
his *Barmitzvah*.

dating back to the Ottoman period,
were added by the Anglo-Jewish
philanthropist Sir Moses Montefiore,
one of Jerusalem's foremost
benefactors. Beneath is an earlier
layer of much larger, uncut stones;
underneath this seven layers of
smoothly chiseled rectangular
limestone blocks with no mortar
between them, dating back to the
Herodian period. Below the ground
are some eighteen or nineteen
further rows of stones before we
reach the foundations.

Contrary to previous thinking, the
Western Wall was never part of the
Temple itself but one of the four
supporting walls built by King
Herod to enlarge the Temple
platform—or maybe even part of the
wall that surrounded the outer
forecourt. Public buildings and small
shops used to stand here, serving the
Jewish pilgrims who streamed to the

Temple three times a year to celebrate the three great religious festivals. The Jewish historian Josephus describes these buildings and the colorful hustle and bustle of festival days.

Visitors to the wall can see scraps of paper thrust into cracks of the wall. Orthodox—and less devout—Jews write special prayers on these notes, addressed to the *Shekinah*, the divine presence supposed to hover above the walls in response to the people's faith.

At the climax of the Jewish calendar, sunset on *Yom Kippur* (the Day of Atonement), when it is believed that God seals the fate of each person for the coming year, thousands stream to the wall to repent before sundown.

As we have seen, the Western Wall is the focus of religious activity for Jews in the Old City. Since the

Left: A Jewish rabbi blows the *shofar* horn at the Western Wall on *Rosh Hashanah*.

Opposite: The masonry of the Western Wall. Many devout Jews place prayers on slips of paper into crannies in the wall.

Speak ye comfortably to Jerusalem

Comfort ye, comfort ye my people, saith your God. Speak ye comfortably to Jerusalem, and cry unto her, that her warfare is accomplished, that her iniquity is pardoned: for she hath received of the LORD's hand double for all her sins.

The voice of him that crieth in the wilderness, Prepare ye the way of the LORD, make straight in the desert a highway for our God. Every valley shall be exalted, and every mountain and hill shall be made low: and the crooked shall be made straight, and the rough places plain: and the glory of the LORD shall be revealed, and all flesh shall see it together: for the mouth of the LORD hath spoken it. The voice said, Cry. And he said, What shall I cry? All flesh is grass, and all the goodliness thereof is as the flower of the field: the grass withereth, the flower fadeth: because the spirit of the LORD bloweth upon it: surely the people is grass. The grass withereth, the flower fadeth: but the word of our God shall stand for ever.

O Zion, that bringest good tidings, get thee up into the high mountain; O Jerusalem, that bringest good tidings, lift up thy voice with strength; lift it up, be not afraid; say unto the cities of Judah, Behold your God! Behold, the Lord GOD will come with strong hand, and his arm shall rule for him: behold, his reward is with him, and his work before him. He shall feed his flock like a shepherd: he shall gather the lambs with his arm, and carry them in his bosom, and shall gently lead those that are with young.

Isaiah 40:1-11

Monument at the Western Wall for Jews killed in the Holocaust.

Opposite: Robinson's Arch, which originally supported massive stairs leading into Herod's Temple. The arch is named after its American discoverer.

Right: The stone pavement in front of the Temple Mount area.

Six-Day War, the Israelis have cleared a huge area in front of the wall. This area, formerly known as the Moors' Quarter, included a mosque and Muslim shrine and was mainly occupied with housing. It was bulldozed to make space for the plaza providing an area for the use of worshipers, for prayer, for special festivals, and religious celebrations.

After the destruction of the Temple

As we have noticed above, the foundations and lower courses of the Western Wall were part of the great platform built to support Herod's Temple. After the destruction of the Temple by the Romans in 70 A.D., the Jews were banned from the city, and the only archaeological evidence uncovered for the succeeding years is of buildings such as bathhouses and bakers' shops built for the use of the occupying Roman Tenth Legion. Gradually, as the restrictions were relaxed and Jews were again permitted into the city, the Western Wall became the focus of Jews coming to lament the loss of the Temple, particular on the 9 Ab.

Archaeological findings

Since 1967 a much greater area of Herodian stonework has been revealed, measuring about 57 meters in length with seven courses of masonry exposed. Excavations have shown that a further nineteen

Right: Partially restored steps which originally led to the gates into Herod's Temple.

courses of Herodian masonry lie underground to a depth of twenty-one meters. These stones, like those of the Herodian Cave of Machpelah in Hebron, are very finely cut from yellowish-gray rock and are positioned without use of mortar between them. The stone blocks vary in size, the largest weighing as much as one hundred tons.

Near the northwest corner of the Western Wall is Wilson's Arch, where a great deal of archaeological excavation has taken place since 1968. It is conjectured that this arch originally formed part of a causeway crossing the Tyropoeon Valley, linking the Upper City with the Temple.

At the southern end of the wall is the huge stone lintel of Barclay's Gate, named after the British Victorian architect who discovered it. It is surmised that this gate originally led from the paved street outside via a ramp into the Temple area.

The archaeological zone

At the southernmost end of the *Haram* are the remains of another huge arch protruding from the Herodian stonework. This is known as Robinson's Arch, after its

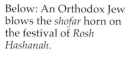
Below: An Orthodox Jew blows the *shofar* horn on the festival of *Rosh Hashanah.*

American discoverer in 1835. At one time it was thought that this arch, like Wilson's, carried a causeway across the Tyropoeon Valley; but it is now more generally believed that the arch supported steps leading from the Lower City up into the Temple Mount. Shops dating from the Herodian period have been discovered in the piers excavated below the arch, together with a Herodian road at the foot of the wall.

Among other fascinating finds in this area has been the southwest cornerstone of the parapet of the Herodian platform, which featured an inscription identifying it as the spot from which the ram's horn, or

shofar, was blown to announce the start of the Sabbath.

The southern end of the wall of the *Haram al Sharif* is now devoted to archaeology and can be visited with a trained guide. This archaeological garden includes fascinating remains dating from the time of Jesus.

Among the intriguing finds is the blocked entrance of a double gate into the Temple Mount area, believed to have formed one of the major approaches to the Temple from the Lower City in Herod the Great's time. Below it ran a wide paved street, reached by a flight of thirty steps. Further east lies another blocked gate, the much larger Triple

Above: A Jew prays at the Western Wall.

Jerusalem shall dwell safely

Behold, the days come, saith the LORD, that I will perform that good thing which I have promised unto the house of Israel and to the house of Judah.

In those days, and at that time, will I cause the Branch of righteousness to grow up unto David; and he shall execute judgment and righteousness in the land. In those days shall Judah be saved, and Jerusalem shall dwell safely: and this is the name wherewith she shall be called, The LORD our righteousness.

Jeremiah 33:14-16

Right: A young man at the Western Wall. He has the *tephillim* containing part of the Law strapped to his forehead.

Gate, again with monumental steps leading to it from the former road below.

A holy place

When the Muslims appropriated the Temple Mount area and built the Dome of the Rock and Aqsa Mosque in the seventh century, they banned Jews from the site. The Western Wall now became the main access point for Jews wishing to approach the Temple area. The Jews continued to have special regard for this place, and when Jews were again allowed to settle in Jerusalem from the thirteenth century, they once more visited the Wall regularly for prayer and lamentation.

Such a practice continued down the centuries, though the area of wall exposed was much smaller than that which we see today. The wall area was about fifty meters long with just five courses of Herodian stonework exposed. The area in front of the wall was also very narrow—less than four

Below: At the Western Wall.

Right: At the women's section of the Western Wall.

Left: A Jewish woman prays at the Western Wall.

Left: Young Jewish boys at the Western Wall.

meters—with the result that the Jewish worshipers were hemmed in tightly by closely built housing.

Although there were several attempts by Jews in the late nineteenth and early twentieth centuries to buy the land near the wall, these failed for lack of funds. Meanwhile, in 1930 a League of Nations ruling judged that the area was a Muslim holy area but that the Jews were to have access for religious purposes. However, after the 1948 war, when the city was divided and this section came under Jordanian rule, the Western Wall became completely inaccessible for Jews from Israel.

The Jewish Quarter

Between the sixteenth and nineteenth centuries the south-central area of the Old City became known as the Jewish Quarter. There had been previous periods when Jews were completely banned from the city—such as immediately following the destruction of the city in 70 A.D.—but from the sixteenth century onward, while the city was under Ottoman rule, the Jewish community gradually increased in numbers. By the late nineteenth century three main groups of Jews were living in the city—the Sephardi (Spanish) Jews, who had arrived in the fifteenth century; the Ashkenazi Jews, who arrived around the end of the seventeenth century from central and East European countries such as Russia, Hungary, Poland, Germany, and Austria; and a small and separate community called the Karaites. The Ashkenazi included a number of Hasidic Jews, known for their strict religious observance.

From the mid-nineteenth century wealthy European Jews, such as the well-known Rothschilds and

Above: Reading the Scriptures at the Western Wall, with *tephillim* strapped to the arm.

Jesus in the Temple

And when [Jesus] was twelve years old, they went up to Jerusalem after the custom of the feast. And when they had fulfilled the days, as they returned, the child Jesus tarried behind in Jerusalem; and Joseph and his mother knew not of it....And it came to pass, that after three days they found him in the temple, sitting in the midst of the doctors.

Luke 2:42,43,46

Right: A *Barmitzvah* at the Western Wall.

Montefiores, tried to improve conditions for the impoverished Jewish community in the city by setting up schools, hospitals, and immigrant housing. However, when the city was divided after the fighting in 1948, the Jews abandoned the Quarter and many of the buildings were destroyed by the Arabs. The area was then used for the settlement of refugees.

Following the reunification of the city of Jerusalem after the Six-Day War of 1967, Israel took control of this area again. As we have seen previously, the Moors' Quarter in front of the Western Wall was destroyed to make way for the great plaza.

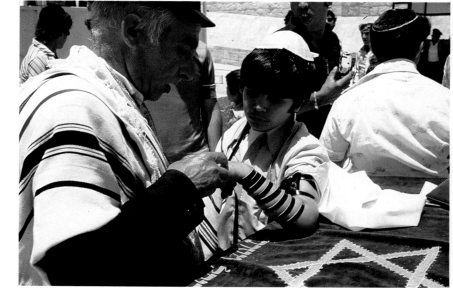

The great destruction wreaked in this area after 1948 has had a fortunate, if unforeseen, outcome. Restoration was clearly urgently needed, once Israel had retaken possession in 1967; but in redeveloping, the archaeologists were given ample opportunity to investigate before the rebuilding started.

The area has been a major focus for archaeological excavation, conservation, and rebuilding, with a policy during the 1980s of settling immigrant Jews here.

The Israelite Tower

Among the fascinating archaeological finds in the Jewish Quarter

Above: A young Jewish boy reads from the Hebrew Scriptures at *Barmitzvah* at the Western Wall. Women of his family have to watch from outside the men's area.

Left: This young boy has the *tephillim* strapped to his forehead at his *Barmitzvah* at the Western Wall.

Opposite: Orthodox Jews
in their characteristic
dark clothing.

Right: An Orthodox
family at the Western
Wall.

was the Israelite Tower, with walls
more than four meters thick, still
standing some eight meters high.
This was possibly part of a gate-
tower in the Israelite city wall of the
seventh century B.C. Signs of burning
and the remains of arrowheads have
also been uncovered at the tower,
probably dating from the disastrous
sacking of the city by Babylon in the
year 586 B.C.

Nearby is another uncovered
stretch of Israelite city wall, which
can be viewed by the visitor. This
wall is about seven meters in
breadth, meriting its name of the
Broad Wall, and probably forms the
foundations of the city wall of the
time of King Hezekiah in the eighth
century B.C.

The Burnt House
Another extraordinary find made in
the excavations undertaken since
1968 was the Burnt House, a wealthy
residence which was evidently
destroyed during the Roman sacking
of the city in 70 A.D. Josephus graphically describes the destruction:
"When they went in numbers into
the lanes of the city, with their
swords drawn, they killed without
mercy those they caught, and set fire
to the house where the Jews had fled,
burning every last person."
Archaeological excavations revealed
a number of household objects and
Below: Orthodox Jews   articles of furniture from the Burnt
come to the Western Wall   House, and these have been restored
to pray.   to appear much as they would have

Opposite: Soldiers pray at the Tomb of David on Mount Zion. Archaeologists cast doubt on this site's identification.

Right: *Torah* scrolls containing the Hebrew Scriptures.

Above: The interior of one of the Sephardic synagogues in the Jewish Quarter.

when in use in the first century A.D., the time of Jesus. Poignantly, the date of the destruction is pinpointed by the find of the latest coin, dating from the year 69 A.D.

The Burnt House can be visited and has a short sound-and-light show to explain its history.

Cardo Maximus

Another fine piece of conservation and reconstruction has been undertaken nearby at the Byzantine *cardo maximus*, a monumental porticoed street probably built by Emperor Justinian (527-65). The street itself was originally some twelve-and-a-half-meters (thirty-six feet) wide, with pavements a further five meters (sixteen feet) in width. Some of the huge columns which lined the street have been re-erected to give a clear idea of the original appearance of the site.

Synagogues

In the Jewish Quarter there was, of course, a large number of synagogues. However, all of them were either badly damaged, or completely destroyed, after the division of the city in 1948. Since 1967 there has been a concerted program for the conservation or rebuilding of many of these synagogues.

The Ramban Synagogue

The oldest synagogue in Jerusalem is the Ramban, which can be traced in origin back to the Jewish scholar Moses ben Nachman, or Nachman-ides, a Talmudic scholar from Spain. When he came to Jerusalem in 1267 he found only two Jews there, so he set about building up a Jewish community.

He initially established a synagogue in a ruined building on Mount Zion, but later moved it to the present site. Rebuilt in 1523, it was closed by the Turkish governor in 1586. The Ramban Synagogue has been refurbished since the Six-Day War and is now in regular use.

The Hurva Synagogue

In the early eighteenth century some Ashkenazi Jews from Poland, led by a one-time follower of the Jewish false messiah Sabbatai Tsvi, tried to build a new synagogue. However, the building was never completed because the Polish Jews fell out with one another after the death of their leader only five days after he arrived in Jerusalem. The group, numbering about 500, represented one of the largest single waves of immigrants before the rise of the modern Zionist movement. They continued to build, depending on cash borrowed from local Muslims to finance the work. When they could no longer repay

their debts, the half-built synagogue was confiscated in lieu of payment by the Muslim money lenders. The synagogue became a ruin—*Hurva* in Hebrew.

In the next century the Turkish Ibrahim Pasha handed back the ruined synagogue to the Ashkenazi community (1838), after which it became generally known as the ruin, or Hurva, Synagogue. The community now set about rebuilding and finally completed the synagogue in 1856. This building rapidly became the center of the Jewish Quarter.

The Hurva Synagogue was destroyed in 1948 by the Arab

Above: Restored remains of the Hurva Synagogue, destroyed in 1948.

Left: Remains of the Synagogue of *Tiferet Israel*, or Glory of Israel, destroyed in 1948.

Legion, but restoration commenced again in 1977. The ruined site is now dominated by a striking, slender stone arch constructed from the ruins. Although there has been much discussion concerning the need to rebuild the synagogue completely, the various religious groups involved cannot come to an agreement on the project.

The Sephardic synagogues
Nearby in the Jewish Quarter are four linked synagogues of the Sephardi community: the ben Zakkai, Elijah, Middle, and Stambouli synagogues. The Sephardic Jews were expelled from Spain and Portugal at the end of the

fifteenth century. Settling at first in the Ottoman Empire, they moved to Palestine almost as soon as the Ottomans took it over in 1516.

The earliest of these four synagogues is the ben Zakkai, built in the opening years of the seventeenth century. The other three synagogues were gradually added to the complex in the following centuries in a rather haphazard fashion. The Elijah Synagogue was originally a study hall, converted into a synagogue in 1702. Although these four synagogues, too, were abandoned after the fighting in 1948, they were left structurally intact by the Arabs. Used as stables in the Jordanian period, they have now

been carefully restored for use. Much of the furnishing has been carried out using fittings salvaged from Italian synagogues wrecked during World War II.

Yeshiva
Also in the Jewish Quarter—as well as in the Orthodox stronghold of Mea Shearim in East Jerusalem—is a number of *Yeshiva*, or Jewish schools, where students study the *Talmud*, the Hebrew and Aramaic commentaries on the *Torah*, the Jewish Law. Many of the members of these *Yeshiva* are hoping to encourage nonobservant Jews to return to their roots and return once again to more traditional, Orthodox Judaism.

Above: At the traditional site of the Tomb of David on Mount Zion.

The LORD doth build up Jerusalem

Praise ye the LORD: for it is good to sing praises unto our God;
  for it is pleasant; and praise is comely.
The LORD doth build up Jerusalem: he gathereth together the outcasts of Israel.
He healeth the broken in heart, and bindeth up their wounds.
He telleth the number of the stars; he calleth them all by their names.
Great is our Lord, and of great power: his understanding is infinite. . . .
Praise the LORD, O Jerusalem; praise thy God, O Zion.
For he hath strengthened the bars of thy gates; he hath blessed thy children within thee.

Psalm 147:1-5,12,13

The Tomb of David

Outside the Jewish Quarter but on a site much revered by the Jewish people is the Tomb of David on Mount Zion, close by the Hall of the Last Supper. Though much regarded by Jews, the site has little or no claim to authenticity. David was buried in David's City on the southeast hill (see 1 Kings 2:10). His tomb has only been claimed to be on this site since as late as the eleventh century A.D. Since 1948 this site has been in Jewish custody and treated as a religious shrine. For the twenty years between 1948 and 1967, during which the Jews had no access to the Western Wall, this became a vital place of Jewish religious observance. The shrine itself contains a cenotaph, or empty grave, draped in heavy, colored cloths.

Above: Part of the so-called Broad Wall; a city wall possibly dating from the time of King Hezekiah in the late eighth century B.C.

Right: Basketball in the Jewish Quarter of the Old City.

Left: Part of the restored Byzantine *cardo maximus*, a monumental porticoed street in the modern Jewish Quarter.

Above: The "Burnt House"—part of a site excavated in 1970 and comprising houses destroyed during the sacking of Jerusalem by the Romans in 70 A.D.

Right: A goldsmith at work in the Jewish Quarter.

Let mount Zion rejoice

Great is the LORD, and greatly to be praised in the city of our God, in the
  mountain of his holiness.

Beautiful for situation, the joy of the whole earth, is mount Zion, on the sides
  of the north, the city of the great King.

God is known in her palaces for a refuge.

For, lo, the kings were assembled, they passed by together.

They saw it, and so they marveled; they were troubled, and hasted away.

Fear took hold upon them there, and pain, as of a woman in travail.

Thou breakest the ships of Tarshish with an east wind.

As we have heard, so have we seen in the city of the LORD of hosts, in the city
  of our God: God will establish it for ever. Selah.

We have thought of thy loving-kindness, O God, in the midst of thy temple.

According to thy name, O God, so is thy praise unto the ends of the earth: thy
  right hand is full of righteousness.

Let mount Zion rejoice, let the daughters of Judah be glad, because of thy
  judgments.

Walk about Zion, and go round about her: tell the towers thereof.

Mark ye well her bulwarks, consider her palaces;
  that ye may tell it to the generation following.

For this God is our God for ever and ever:
  he will be our guide even unto death.

Psalm 48

5

A Hundred Gates

"For the LORD hath chosen Zion; he hath desired it for his habitation."
(Psalm 132:13)

An Orthodox Jewish scholar copies the *Torah*.

Mea Shearim

Mea Shearim, just outside the Old City, is the center of the ultraorthodox Jewish community in Jerusalem—often known as the *Hasidim*, or *haredim* ("God-fearing"). The migration of Orthodox Jews to Palestine began in the eighteenth century when Rabbi Vilna Gaon taught his followers in Lithuania on the Baltic that the Messiah would not come until the Jews returned to Jerusalem. It was this message that precipitated the migration of many ultraconservative Jews from Eastern Europe to Palestine in succeeding years.

For these migrants, it seemed particularly important to settle within the precincts of the Old City itself—that area alone seemed to promise fulfillment of the prophecy of the Messiah's coming. At first they opposed bitterly the enterprise of other Jewish groups to build new neighborhoods outside the Old City. At the same time, the *haredim* were anxious to avoid the tendency they saw of less strict Jews' assimilating with the local population.

Eventually, and possibly largely to avoid being contaminated by or assimilated with less devout Jews and Gentiles, they built the

neighborhood of Mea Shearim, which from the outset was positively fortress-like in its conception.

A hundred gates

The Hebrew words *Mea Shearim* literally mean "a hundred gates"; when the district was first set up in 1874, it was possible to enter only through the gates—often said to number one hundred. But the name is also a play on the words "a hundredfold." The week the

neighborhood was founded by a meeting of settlers in November 1873, the *Torah* text happened to be Genesis 26:12: "And Isaac sowed in that land, and reaped in the same year a hundredfold. The Lord blessed him." Accordingly, the community took this as its name. Houses were constructed in Mea Shearim after this decision had been taken, and were originally provided with communal kitchen and toilet facilities. They still boast a

Jerusalem—above my chief joy

By the rivers of Babylon, there we sat down, yea,
   we wept, when we remembered Zion.

We hanged our harps upon the willows in the
   midst thereof.

For there they that carried us away captive
   required of us a song; and they that wasted us
   required of us mirth, saying, Sing us one of the
   songs of Zion.

How shall we sing the LORD's song in a strange
   land?

If I forget thee, O Jerusalem, let my right hand
   forget her cunning.

If I do not remember thee, let my tongue cleave to
   the roof of my mouth;

   if I prefer not Jerusalem above my chief joy.

Psalm 137:1-6

communal bread oven.

When it was completed, the area was the largest single private building project in Jerusalem. It is now a center for Jewish books, religious articles, and scribes. There are also many shops offering craftsmen's artifacts and beautiful silverware, as well as kosher food shops. Many synagogues and *Torah* schools, or *Yeshiva*, are also found in this area, as well as ritual baths, or *mikveh*.

It is clear immediately on entering the area that it is different. It is like entering the ghetto of one of the East European cities during the eighteenth or nineteenth century. Whatever the weather, the men wear long black overcoats and black

Above: Students at the *Yeshiva*.

Below: Orthodox Jewish children at school.

Opposite: Making a prayer shawl.

Jerusalem a city of truth

Thus saith the LORD*; I am returned unto Zion, and will dwell in the midst of Jerusalem: and Jerusalem shall be called a city of truth; and the mountain of the* LORD *of hosts the holy mountain.*

Zechariah 8:3

broad-brimmed hats. Many have long beards, and most also have long side curls (*peiyot*) hanging from beneath their hats. Some men wear black breeches and white stockings—a hangover from the 18th century—and, on the Sabbath, these men substitute for their workday headgear the fur-rimmed round hats known as *shtreimels*.

The women, too, dress distinctively. Their dress is modest—long skirts, long sleeves, and high collars. Married women often have shaven heads, covered in public by a wig or scarf.

A holy language

The residents of Mea Shearim speak mainly Yiddish—a language made up of elements of German, Polish, Russian, and Hebrew, reflecting the original countries of these immigrants. They regard Hebrew as a holy language whose use should be restricted to religious services.

Not surprisingly, the residents of Mea Shearim are critical of visitors who are casually and inadequately dressed. Notices inform tourists and others: "We do not tolerate people passing through our streets immodestly dressed," and notices at access points to the area ask that the traditions of the Orthodox residents be respected.

Below: The schoolbus.

Right: An Orthodox Jew in a deserted Jerusalem street.

Opposite: An Orthodox Jew.

The busiest day of the week in Mea Shearim is Friday. Everyone is bustling about in preparation for the Sabbath, when no work at all must be done. The men must go to the ritual bath, or *mikveh*, and the women must buy food for the following day. On the Sabbath itself, Mea Shearim becomes a haven of rest; all traffic is prohibited.

The streets of Jerusalem

Thus saith the LORD *of hosts; There shall yet old men and old women dwell in the streets of Jerusalem, and every man with his staff in his hand for very age. And the streets of the city shall be full of boys and girls playing in the streets thereof. Thus saith the* LORD *of hosts: If it be marvelous in the eyes of the remnant of this people in these days, should it also be marvelous in mine eyes? saith the* LORD *of hosts.*

Zechariah 8:4-6

Opposite: Stained glass window in the Synagogue of the High Rabbinate, King George St. Renanim, with an artist's impression of Herod's Temple.

Right: Interior of the Synagogue of the High Rabbinate, King George St. Renanim.

PRESENTED BY MR JACK H AND MRS REINHARDT
IN LOVING MEMORY OF THEIR PARENTS

I will save my people

Thus saith the LORD of hosts; Behold, I will save my people from the east country, and from the west country; and I will bring them, and they shall dwell in the midst of Jerusalem: and they shall be my people, and I will be their God, in truth and in righteousness.

Zechariah 8:7,8

Opposite: A Torah scribe.

Left: Stained glass window depicting the Menorah, in the Renanim Synagogue.

Below: Copying the *Torah*.

Above: Interior of the Jerusalem Great Synagogue.

I will rejoice in Jerusalem

For, behold, I create new heavens and a new earth: and the former shall not be remembered, nor come into mind. But be ye glad and rejoice for ever in that which I create: for, behold, I create Jerusalem a rejoicing, and her people a joy. And I will rejoice in Jerusalem, and joy in my people: and the voice of weeping shall be no more heard in her, nor the voice of crying. There shall be no more thence an infant of days, nor an old man that hath not filled his days: for the child shall die a hundred years old; but the sinner being a hundred years old shall be accursed. And they shall build houses, and inhabit them; and they shall plant vineyards, and eat the fruit of them. They shall not build, and another inhabit; they shall not plant, and another eat: for as the days of a tree are the days of my people, and mine elect shall long enjoy the work of their hands.

Isaiah 65:17-22

6

Jesus and Jerusalem

"O Jerusalem, Jerusalem . . . how often would I have gathered thy children together."
(Matthew 23:37)

'Ain Karim, traditional birthplace of John the Baptist.

Opposite: The Mount of Olives from the village of Bethphage, where Jesus' Palm Sunday entry into Jerusalem commenced (Mark 11:1).

Opposite (far right): Christians retrace Jesus' path down the Mount of Olives on Palm Sunday.

Right: Christian pilgrims with palms celebrate Palm Sunday outside the walls of the Old City.

Places of Jesus' Passion

Blessed be the King!

And it came to pass, when he was come nigh to Bethphage and Bethany, at the mount called the mount of Olives, he sent two of his disciples, saying, Go ye into the village over against you; in the which at your entering ye shall find a colt tied, whereon yet never man sat: loose him, and bring him hither. . . . And they that were sent went their way, and found even as he had said unto them. And as they were loosing the colt, the owners thereof said unto them, Why loose ye the colt? And they said, The Lord hath need of him. And they brought him to Jesus: and they cast their garments upon the colt, and they set Jesus thereon. And as he went, they spread their clothes in the way. And when he was come nigh, even now at the descent of the mount of Olives, the whole multitude of the disciples began to rejoice and praise God with a loud voice for all the mighty works that they had seen; saying, Blessed be the King that cometh in the name of the Lord: peace in heaven, and glory in the highest.
Luke 19:29,30,32-38

In this chapter we look at some of the sites connected closely with the events of the last week of Jesus' earthly life, in the sequence in which they appear in the Gospel story. We look not so much at the churches—they have largely been covered earlier in chapter 3—but at the places themselves and at their claims to authenticity.

For the Christian, the city of Jerusalem is of paramount interest as the place where Jesus spent the last climactic days of his earthly life, and

Previous spread: The Hall of the Last Supper, or *Coenaculum*, on Mount Zion, built around the twelfth century A.D. on the traditional site of Jesus' Last Supper with his apostles.

Opposite: Ancient olive trees in the walled garden on the site of Gethsemane. It has been estimated that these trees are between 300 and 1000 years old.

Right: Mosaic on the facade of the Church of All Nations, or Church of the Agony, showing Jesus suffering in the Garden of Gethsemane. The church was completed in 1924.

Opposite: An ancient
olive tree in the Garden
of Gethsemane.

At Gethsemane

*Then cometh Jesus with them unto a place
called Gethsemane, and saith unto the
disciples, Sit ye here, while I go and pray
yonder. And he took with him Peter and the
two sons of Zebedee, and began to be
sorrowful and very heavy. Then said he
unto them, My soul is exceeding sorrowful,
even unto death: tarry ye here, and watch
with me. And he went a little farther, and
fell on his face, and prayed, saying, O my
Father, if it be possible, let this cup pass
from me: nevertheless not as I will, but as
thou wilt.*

Matthew 26:36-39

Right: The Garden of
Gethsemane, at the foot
of the Mount of Olives.

where he was crucified and rose again. Christian pilgrims and tourists visiting Jerusalem for the first time are often understandably bewildered by the multiplicity of shrines and churches and baffled as to which sites might have some real claim to authenticity. Often, despairing of knowing if any particular site is authentic, the pilgrim can be tempted to doubt every claim, making do with some such generalization as "Jesus must have seen this landscape," or "Jesus certainly walked this way." Such a reaction, while very natural, is unnecessarily pessimistic.

Using three sources—the Bible, Christian tradition, and archaeology, we can in fact know a great deal about the Jerusalem of Jesus' time and the places he knew. Although the Gospels were not written to be biographies in the modern sense, giving precise details of every aspect of Jesus' life, we can in fact find in

Right: The Pavement, or *Gabbatha* in Aramaic, believed by some to be the place mentioned in John 19:13 where Pontius Pilate sat in judgment on Jesus. Games have been scribed into the pavement's surface, and were posssibly played by Roman soldiers.

the Gospels much evidence about contemporary Jerusalem, its life and people. Certain events are described as taking place in specific named places—at the Pool of Bethesda, the Garden of Gethsemane, or Solomon's Porch, for example.

But possibly more useful for deciding whether places pointed out to visitors are what they are claimed to be is early Christian tradition. For example, we know that from very early times—only a few years after the death of Jesus—certain sites were already associated with critical events in his life and were often visited for religious services that commemorated those events. By the time of the first recorded Christian pilgrim's visit to Jerusalem in 333 A.D. there was already a large number of sites confidently linked with the events in Passion Week.

Finally, archaeology can shed further light on the matter. Although the climatic conditions mean that few organic remains have survived in this region, we do have plentiful remains of buildings—particularly the larger, more durable monuments such as Herod's Temple. With the ever-increasing refinement of archaeological skills and the enormous efforts put into excavations since 1967, a great deal is now known of the overall history of Jerusalem—and of Jerusalem in the time of Jesus.

Bethphage

Modern Palm Sunday processions, held annually in the city of Jerusalem, set off from the Latin church of Bethphage. The Bible says that Jesus was near "Bethphage and Bethany, at the mount of Olives" (Mark 11:1) when he sent off two disciples to the nearby village to procure a donkey. It is unclear exactly where biblical Bethphage was situated; in early times it was believed to be on the site of the modern Arab village of et-Tur. However, the present church of Bethphage, a Franciscan monastery dating from the nineteenth century, stands on the site of a twelfth-century church, by tradition built on the site of the biblical Bethphage. The medieval church included a stone that the Crusaders believed Jesus used to mount his donkey—forgetting that he was mounting a little donkey, not a full-grown horse.

From Bethphage the Palm Sunday processions march to the crown of the Mount of Olives and then down the hill, entering the Old City by St. Stephen's Gate.

The Hall of the Last Supper

The so-called Hall of the Last Supper, often known by its Latin name as the *Coenaculum*, or "Cenacle," is found on Mount Zion just outside the city walls. By the fourth century there was a strong Christian tradition that this was the site of the house with the Upper Room, where Jesus and his twelve disciples celebrated the Last Supper together (Mark 14:15). It was also believed to be the site of the House of Caiaphas, the high priest, to which Jesus was taken after his arrest in Gethsemane and where Peter three times denied him; and also the site of the house where, after the ascension, the disciples gathered on the Day of Pentecost and the Holy Spirit descended on them. Not only this, but it was also held to be the site of the house of Mary, the mother of John Mark, where Peter came after his release by angels from prison; and finally it was believed to be the place where Mary died.

The Hall of the Last Supper, probably built in the twelfth century and restored in the fourteenth by Latin architects introduced by the Franciscans, stands over this supposed site of the Last Supper. This is a particularly unreliable tradition and seems to derive from the better-based belief that this was

Behold your King!

Pilate therefore . . . brought Jesus forth, and sat down in the judgment seat in a place that is called the Pavement, but in the Hebrew, Gabbatha. And it was the preparation of the passover, and about the sixth hour: and he saith unto the Jews, Behold your King! But they cried out, Away with him, Away with him, crucify him. Pilate saith unto them, Shall I crucify your King? The chief priests answered, We have no king but Caesar. Then delivered he him therefore unto them to be crucified. And they took Jesus, and led him away.
John 19:13–16

Opposite: The Dormition Church on Mount Zion, by tradition the place where Mary died.

Right: Steps dating probably from the Byzantine period, near St. Peter in Gallicantu.

Peter's denial

And as Peter was beneath in the palace, there cometh one of the maids of the high priest: and when she saw Peter warming himself, she looked upon him, and said, And thou also wast with Jesus of Nazareth. But he denied, saying, I know not, neither understand I what thou sayest. And he went out into the porch; and the cock crew.
Mark 14:66-68

Right: Steps near St. Peter in Gallicantu.

the place where the Holy Spirit descended upon the disciples at Pentecost. At some point the two upper rooms seem to have been merged.

Gethsemane
The Gospels tell us that after the Last Supper and the singing of a hymn, Jesus and his disciples went out across the Kidron Valley to a place on the Mount of Olives where there was a garden, a place called Gethsemane. We know that Jesus had often met there with his disciples (John 18:2), and there may have been shelter—it was cold on that particular evening (John 18:18).

Opposite: This place is known as the Place of the Skull, or Golgotha, as it is held to resemble a human skull, with two caves serving as eye sockets.

Although we would not expect to find archaeological remains for a garden, or "orchard" (John 18:1, Moffatt translation) and therefore might wonder if we could truly identify this site, in fact its name has never gone out of use and the general area of its location is in no doubt. There is little reason to doubt the identification of Gethsemane (meaning "oil press") with the area

Above: General Gordon (of Khartoum) believed this site above the modern bus station of East Jerusalem to be the authentic location of Golgotha.

at or near the Church of the Agony, mentioned previously. However, it is most unlikely that the ancient olive trees carefully maintained in the Franciscan garden are much more than 1000 years old or that they date from the time of Jesus.

The Pavement
After Jesus' arrest in Gethsemane, he was taken for trial by the high

priest's guards. As we know from the Gospels, after a hearing before the Jewish Sanhedrin, Jesus was taken to the Roman governor, or prefect, Pontius Pilate, for judgment. Although various sites for the prefect's residence, or Praetorium, have been suggested, it now seems that the most likely place is what we know as the Citadel, where Herod the Great had built an impressive

Right: The Cenacle, or Hall of the Last Supper, on Mount Zion.

Opposite: The Garden Tomb, first identified as Jesus' tomb by General Gordon in 1883, has no early tradition to support its authenticity. However, many Christian find its atmosphere helps them remember the Gospel story well.

Right: Christian tourists gather outside the Garden Tomb.

Right: Interior of the Garden Tomb, which originally contained three projecting benches.

palace. It appears that the trial took place outside in the open, with Pilate sitting on a platform (*bema*) (Matthew 27:19), with sentence delivered from a seat "in the place called *Lithostroton*, but in Hebrew *Gabbatha*" (John 19:13), and not at the Antonia Fortress, where a pavement is displayed to visitors as the likely location of the trial (see p. 156).

St. Peter in Gallicantu

Also on Mount Zion is the Church of St. Peter in Gallicantu—that is, St. Peter's-at-the-place-where-the-cock-crew. The present church is a modern building constructed by the Assumptionist Fathers in 1928-32, but it stands over older remains. Tradition has it that this is the site of the House of Caiaphas, where Jesus was taken following his arrest, and outside which Peter wept so bitterly after three times denying he knew Jesus (Matthew 26:75).

However, this is unlikely to be the site of Caiaphas' house, since it almost certainly stood outside the city walls of that time; and we know that in the time of Jesus the wealthier citizens' houses were mainly situated at the top of the hill. Nevertheless, as early as the fourth century pilgrims were visiting this as the authentic site, and continued to do so thereafter. When the foundations for the present church were being excavated, a variety of walls, steps, tombs, and mosaics dating from the Herodian period were uncovered in and around the site. Near the church is an old flight of steps, possibly from the Byzantine period, leading from the lower city to the upper city of that time.

He is risen!

Now upon the first day of the week, very early in the morning, they came unto the sepulchre, bringing the spices which they had prepared, and certain others with them. And they found the stone rolled away from the sepulchre. And they entered in, and found not the body of the Lord Jesus. And it came to pass, as they were much perplexed thereabout, behold, two men stood by them in shining garments: and as they were afraid, and bowed down their faces to the earth, they said unto them, Why seek ye the living among the dead? He is not here, but is risen.
Luke 24:1-6a

Above: On the ancient steps near St. Peter in Gallicantu.

Previous spread: The Tomb of the Herod family in Bloomfield Park has a huge rolling stone door, similar to that which the Gospels describe as protecting Jesus' tomb.

Gordon's Calvary

There is a prominent knoll or hillock behind the East Jerusalem bus station where the rock is bare. Popular belief has held that this is the "place of the skull" (Golgotha), since the rock is held to resemble a skull, with two dark caves suggesting the eye sockets. Apparently in support of this suggestion was the Jewish tradition that the place of crucifixion was outside the city (as the well-known hymn, "There is a green hill far away . . . ," reflects) on the Damascus Road. Grasping these two points, several nineteenth-century writers, including Conder in 1878, identified this site as the true Calvary.

The eccentric British General Charles Gordon, later of Khartoum fame, became intrigued with the problem of identifying the holy sites. He adopted this hypothesis as it fitted with his other claim—that what is now known as the Garden Tomb was the authentic tomb of Jesus. Looking across the northern wall of the Old City, he noted the skull-like features of Skull Hill and then discovered the tomb just below the cliff.

Not least of the arguments against the authenticity of this site is that the configuration of the caves on the cliff has changed over the two millennia since the death of Christ; we have no

reason to believe that in Jesus' day the cliff did resemble a skull.

The Garden Tomb

The Garden Tomb is cut into a quarry face and is situated in what is now a beautifully kept garden. A door and windows were added to the tomb after its first construction—probably in Byzantine or Crusader times. Inside the tomb is a square chamber with three projecting benches which have been severely damaged. In 1883 Gordon claimed this tomb to be the sepulchre of Christ, but there is no early tradition

whatever to support his claim. Moreover, if the cliff Gordon claimed to be Golgotha is inauthentic, there is little evidence to support the identification of the Garden Tomb as Jesus' burial place.

Gordon wrote up his discovery in the pages of the *Palestine Exploration Fund Quarterly*, and so great was the interest raised that he gathered sufficient funds to buy the neighboring garden in the following year, 1884. Later excavations uncovered a water cistern and wine press on the site.

Because of its peaceful atmosphere

and pleasant ambience, many tourists and other visitors incline to treat the Garden Tomb as authentic, finding it more amenable to devotion than the dark and noisy interior of the Church of the Holy Sepulchre, which in fact has a much stronger claim to authenticity. The Garden Tomb is open daily except Sundays.

Aceldama

The site now known as Aceldama, in the Hinnom Valley, has been known as the "field of blood" since the time of the Christian historian Eusebius c. 330 A.D. This may be because the chief priests bought it with the blood money thrown back at them by Judas—or because Judas Iscariot actually committed suicide on this site (Matthew 27:7-10; Acts 1:18,19). Certainly we know that the southern part of the field became a place to bury strangers, as the relevant verses in Matthew's Gospel state.

The site is marked by the Greek Convent of St. Onuphrius, an Egyptian hermit celebrated for the length of his beard. He eventually let it grow so long that he had need of no other covering to preserve his modesty!

The New Jerusalem

This phrase occurs only twice in the Bible, at the beginning and end of the Book of Revelation. In Revelation 21 an angel takes St. John the Divine to the top of a mountain and shows him the New Jerusalem, a description of which John affords us in the following verses. He gives a detailed description—of its size, the materials from which it is made, and its means of illumination. He explains that there is no temple, no sun or moon, no night, no closing of its gates, and no evil in the New Jerusalem.

But what is the New Jerusalem?

Above: Aceldama, or "Field of Blood," by tradition the field Judas Iscariot bought with the silver after betraying Jesus, and where he hung himself (Acts 1:18,19).

Right: The Damascus
Gate.

The Old Jerusalem was the place
where God's rule over his people
and his presence was centered; the
New Jerusalem will be the home of
the new, greater people of God. This
New Jerusalem is the home of all
God's believing people—Jews and
Gentiles—from Old and New
Testament times.

Revelation 21 states that the New
Jerusalem is a "holy city . . . coming
down from God out of heaven,
prepared as a bride adorned for her
husband." Christians understand
John's description in different ways.
Some believe it to be a literal,
material city, which will appear as a
gigantic cube at the beginning of the
millennium—the 1000-year earthly

Right: The modern
approach to the
Damascus Gate, one of
the busiest entrances to
the city.

The Holy City

*And I saw a new heaven and a new earth: for the first heaven and the
first earth were passed away; and there was no more sea. And I John saw
the holy city, new Jerusalem, coming down from God out of heaven,
prepared as a bride adorned for her husband. And I heard a great voice
out of heaven saying, Behold, the tabernacle of God is with men, and he
will dwell with them, and they shall be his people, and God himself shall
be with them, and be their God. And God shall wipe away all tears from
their eyes; and there shall be no more death, neither sorrow, nor crying,
neither shall there be any more pain: for the former things are passed
away.*
Revelation 21:1-4

Left: St. Stephen's Gate—by tradition the site of Stephen's martyrdom.

reign of Christ. Others believe John is describing the city as it will be in eternity—understanding the details either literally or symbolically. Yet many other Christians take it that the New Jerusalem which John describes is the ideal city of God, which exists not only in the future but also in the present. It is a spiritual entity—not material—and is always "coming down . . . out of heaven."

However they interpret the detail, all Christians see the New Jerusalem as the community of Christ and his people, which will only appear in its perfection when the present age has ended. At the same time, Christians already belong to this spiritual community, which gives them hope for the present and for the age to come.

Left: A busy street in Arab East Jerusalem.

Right: The Russian
Orthodox Cathedral of
the Holy Trinity in the
old Russian compound,
north of the Jaffa Road.

The New Jerusalem

And the twelve gates were twelve pearls: every several gate was of one pearl: and the street of the city was pure gold, as it were transparent glass. And I saw no temple therein: for the Lord God Almighty and the Lamb are the Temple of it. And the city had no need of the sun, neither of the moon, to shine in it: for the glory of God did lighten it, and the Lamb is the light thereof. And the nations of them which are saved shall walk in the light of it: and the kings of the earth do bring their glory and honor into it.

Revelation 21:21-24

7

City of Gold, Copper, and Light

"The LORD loveth the gates of Zion."
(Psalm 87:2)

Stained-glass window depicting guns and shells beaten into plowshares;
from the Ardon Windows, Jerusalem (reproduced by kind permission).

Jerusalem and the arts

One of Israel's most popular folk songs celebrates Jerusalem as a city of gold, copper, and light. These words accurately describe the sight presented by Jerusalem's walls and buildings. Understandably, gold and copper are hard to come by, and have actually been used for only a handful of the numerous cupolas that go to make up Jerusalem's skyline—the most famous being the Dome of the Rock, one of Jerusalem's most beautiful landmarks, and the domes of the Russian churches in the Russian compound and on the Mount of Olives.

The stones of Jerusalem

As forests are scarce around Jerusalem, the principal building material has always been Jerusalem limestone, quarried in the Judean hills and still the predominant feature of Jerusalem's modern architecture. For most of the year Jerusalem enjoys bright blue skies and, as the stone's very pale, almost white color reflects the gleaming sunlight, Jerusalem appears to be truly a city of light. When the sun sets, its glowing red and orange rays seem to cover Jerusalem's ancient walls with gold.

Shortly after the British took

Below: The famous Bezalel School of Art.

Jerusalem from the Turks in 1917, the British governor Sir Ronald Storrs enacted a bylaw requiring square, dressed natural stone for all building projects in Jerusalem. Thanks to this regulation, Jerusalem stone has remained the material for almost all

the city's residential, administrative, and commercial buildings. Following Israel's independence in 1948, the Jerusalem municipality continued to enforce this law. Thus, Jerusalem's unique cityscape was preserved and most new building

projects blend harmoniously and gracefully with their surroundings.

The most powerful argument for using Jerusalem limestone for construction might be the Old City's Jewish Quarter. Following the Jordanian occupation in 1948, all of this quarter's fifty-eight synagogues and most of its houses were demolished and left in ruins for the next nineteen years. After the Old City fell into Israeli hands in 1967, a huge, long-term reconstruction project started. Apart from the wholesale rebuilding of the Jewish Quarter, services necessary for any twentieth-century residential area, such as telecommunications, water, and electricity had to be introduced, while aesthetic requirements had to be satisfied simultaneously.

The Jewish Quarter

Today the Jewish Quarter is one of the most beautiful residential areas in Israel. Its buildings have been beautifully restored, matching what remained of the old walls with newly hewn Jerusalem stone so that it is almost impossible to discern where the old finishes and the new starts. Small, picturesque courtyards lead off the narrow streets and pathways, which have been beautifully laid with new paving stones. Here and there are fragments of the old paving stones discovered in deeper strata and now incorporated into the new surface. On the famous *Via Dolorosa*, some stones may even be those over which the procession to Golgotha walked in 33 A.D., representing precious relics for the many Christian pilgrims visiting Jerusalem. During the period of Jordanian rule, the Old City's thick stone walls from the Ottoman period were disfigured by fortifications. These have now been restored along their entire four-kilometer (two-and-a-half-mile) circumference. Crumbling stones had to be replaced and the walls protected against the seepage of rainwater.

Below: The artist Du-Du Harel at work in his Jerusalem studio.

Opposite: The private museum in honor of President Ben Swil.

Left: The delicate task of reconstructing the Dead Sea Scrolls.

Far left: An expert pieces together fragments of the Dead Sea Scrolls.

Left: The Rockefeller Museum, opened in 1938.

Suburban neighborhoods

Outside the Old City, modern Jerusalem consists of dozens of neighborhoods, each with a distinctive character that is often based on the ethnic background of its residents. When asked where they live, Jerusalemites tend to name their neighborhood rather than give a street address.

Expansion beyond the Old City began during the second half of the nineteenth century. The first neighborhoods outside the walls were built by Jews, who were then the fastest-growing part of the population and were seeking to escape the overcrowded conditions of the Jewish Quarter.

The first of these neighborhoods, Mishkenot Sha'ananim, emerged in 1860 on the other side of the valley opposite the Old City walls. Thirty years later, the Yemin Moshe quarter was built next to it. Both neighborhoods were restored a few decades ago; Mishkenot Sha'ananim has been converted into a guest house for visiting artists, and Yemin Moshe is now largely an artists' colony as well as one of Jerusalem's most prestigious neighborhoods, from which cars are banned.

The neighborhood of Nahlat Shiva followed in 1869 when its seven founders—all sons of rabbis—built small houses along Jaffa Road. Today it has become a unique pedestrian mall and its cobblestone streets are lined with cafés, restaurants, shops, and galleries. In 1874 Mea Shearim was built—at that time the largest neighborhood outside the Old City. Today its crowded dwellings with their small courtyards and narrow pathways are inhabited by ultraorthodox Jews.

The Bucharan

At the end of the nineteenth century the Bucharan Quarter was begun. Built by rich Jews from Buchara and Tashkent (Uzbekistan) as a summer residence, it is fundamentally different from other Jewish neighborhoods. The quarter contains several magnificent houses whose gates, doors, and walls often feature the Star of David to indicate their inhabitants' Jewishness, which they could not openly express in their homeland. The most impressive of these houses is Yehudahoff Mansion, at 19 Ezra Street, built in 1904-05, and which has nearly thirty rooms. Its extraordinary dimensions and its stately, almost Baroque facade with richly ornamented, arched windows earned it the nickname of "the palace."

In 1921, the Rehavia neighborhood was built by affluent European Jews. Most of its buildings were designed by the prominent German architect Eric Mendelssohn, who also designed the Hebrew University building and the Hadassah Hospital on Mount Scopus. Rehavia's one- or two-family homes are surrounded by private gardens, whose mature trees usually help to shade the buildings.

All these early neighborhoods consist predominantly of one- and two-story buildings, and their style blends easily into Jerusalem's urban landscape.

Traditionally, stone was used as the load-bearing component in building. But under British influence during the Mandate period, building technology advanced and construction in concrete started to come into use. Stone was still used to face the walls of buildings, but the weight of the walls and ceilings was now borne by a concrete framework.

Building boom

After World War II and upon Jerusalem's becoming Israel's capital, a period of hectic building activity began. In the divided city East Jerusalem stagnated, but West Jerusalem experienced a building boom with all the associated problems. The city had rapidly to be provided with all the facilities required by a modern capital; and the need to house waves of immigrants from Europe, North Africa, and the Near East led to the development of the first modern suburbs.

This led to a number of problems. Modern urban planning principles and aesthetic and architectural concepts were pushed aside as demand increased for public housing at affordable cost. Huge (and ugly) apartment blocks sprang up around the city with little regard for whether they fit into the existing urban landscape.

Fortunately, the principle of using Jerusalem stone was largely observed, so damage was limited. There are, of course, a few exceptions to this rule: Jerusalem does have some buildings constructed of other building materials, such as the dome-shaped synagogue on the Hebrew University's Giv'at Ram campus, built in the 1960s and made

Right: The Scroll of Isaiah holds the place of honor in the Shrine of the Book, built to house the Dead Sea Scrolls.

of concrete painted white; and the Ein Karem branch of the Hadassah Hospital, constructed of red brick and concrete and presenting a rather ungainly appearance. Other isolated concrete buildings were erected in various parts of Jerusalem, usually during times of economic crisis or shortage of stone.

Kiryat Hayovel, built in the 1950s, was Jerusalem's first example of modern mass housing and has all the drabness associated with budgetary constraints. Its buildings are made of cheap stone and lots of concrete, and the neighborhood stands out as a sore spot in Jerusalem's panorama.

Compared with other modern

Left: The Shrine of the Book, built to resemble the lid of a jar containing the Dead Sea Scrolls.

Opposite: "Jacob's
Ladder."

Right: "The Great Cone"
by the artist Helen
Escobedo (1985).

cities, Jerusalem has comparatively few high-rise buildings. The first of them rose during the period of rather unsupervised building activities during the early 1950s and the 1960s.

Big hotels shot up, as well as commercial buildings such as the City Tower, which houses numerous shops and offices and the Jerusalem Convention Center, Binyanei Ha'ooma, which is a large, rather

bombastic block of a building that greets travelers arriving in Jerusalem from the west. At least these buildings serve as landmarks and are helpful for orientation within the city.

The Israel Museum
By contrast, Israel's national museum, the Israel Museum, provides a more positive example of

Jerusalem's architecture during this period. An international competition for the building's design was won by two Jerusalem architects: Professor Mansfeld and Dora Gad. As a result, they created a unique complex which was made up of separate, interlocking, flat pavilions spread over the hill and unfolding naturally like some traditional Mediterranean village.

Previous spread: The
Music Hall, Jerusalem.

Right: A Henry Moore
sculpture at the Museum
of Modern Art.

Right: Sculptures at the
Museum of Modern Art.

The Jerusalem Committee

After 1967 a more unified planning
approach was developed for the
entire city. As another accelerated
phase of urban development was
under way, finding the best
relationship between the old and the
new was among the most important
problems for planning Jerusalem.
Since experience in these matters
was still lacking in Jerusalem, Mayor
Teddy Kollek invited about seventy
internationally known figures—
architects, city planners, historians,
and philosophers—to follow the

city's development with recom-
mendations and criticism. In this
way the Jerusalem Committee was
founded and ever since has met
every two years, playing a vital role
in Jerusalem's urban development.

The following two decades saw a
very rapid increase in population.
Western Jerusalem grew from
200,000 inhabitants in 1967 to 320,000
in 1985. This is one of the reasons for
the emergence around Jerusalem of
two concentric rings of new suburbs
made up of modern apartment
blocks. The first of those rings was

finished in the mid-1970s; the
second, larger ring was finished in
the 1980s and comprises four
suburbs: Gilo, East Talpiot, Neve
Ya'acov, and Ramot Allon, planned
for a total of 120,000 inhabitants.

The other reason these suburbs
were erected was strategic: They
prevent any redivision of the city.
On the eastern side of Jerusalem, for
example, the new neighborhoods
present a land bridge linking the city
with Mount Scopus, which had been
cut off during the years of the
Jordanian occupation.

Left: A Henry Moore sculpture in front of the Hebrew University buildings.

Left: The Kennedy Memorial.

These new suburbs are mostly inhabited by new immigrants and young families attracted by the more affordable housing costs. Most are strictly dormitory communities, but lately have begun to develop their own character. As is often true of mass housing, great areas of the suburbs are composed of apartment blocks whose architecture frequently reflects the dilemma faced by planners and designers who have to meet functional requirements while trying not to neglect aesthetics.

The neighborhood of Ramot Allon,

for example, erected in north-western Jerusalem—and still expanding—is a mixture of successfully designed one-family homes with small gardens and of densely built apartment blocks. Attempts to make these surroundings a little more interesting with some "original" architecture resulted in a few strange buildings—such as the beehive-like apartment building next to Ramot Allon's main road—which to some represent mere oddities, and to others an outrage.

A more uniform architectural design was achieved in the neigh-borhood of Gilo at Jerusalem's southern edge. This area is densely populated, too, but a better compromise between the functional and the aesthetic has been achieved. Although a few Oriental features such as arches have been used, they are in moderation and add to the neighborhood's relative attractiveness, rather than overwhelming it. The stone used is of a better and more uniform quality in Gilo than that in Ramot Allon.

Right: The library of the
Hebrew University.

The most successful results in matching traditional local architecture with new construction methods were achieved in Talpiot on the eastern side of the city. Large and impersonal apartment blocks were largely avoided, making it a pleasant and airy neighborhood.

East Jerusalem
Unlike the situation in West Jerusalem, construction activity in East Jerusalem stagnated between 1948 and 1967. The main branches of many businesses, as well as government offices, moved to Amman. The only building projects worth mentioning are the commercial center in the triangle between Wadi Joz, the Damascus Gate, and Salah-ed-Din Street, and a

few residential areas in the neighborhoods of Abu Tor and Sheikh Jarrah.

Arab families prefer detached private homes and, in response to Jerusalem's hilly landscape, these houses are often built on pillars. The ground floor usually consists of a paved entrance court, a sun porch, and a large central living room; while the upstairs dwelling unit has a separate entrance which can be reached via an external staircase that also leads to the flat roof.

In the two decades following the city's reunification in 1967, Jerusalem's Arab population more than doubled. The resultant overcrowding caused an increased demand for housing and a tremendous acceleration in

disorganized, haphazard development. Small Arab villages surrounding Jerusalem were swallowed up to become part of the city, and most development concentrated in semi-urban areas such as A-Tur, El-Azariah, and Silwan in the eastern part of Jerusalem, Isawiya near Mount Scopus, and Beit Hanina and Shu'afat in Jerusalem's north, as well as adjacent rural areas.

Until recently these areas had no orderly planning since, for generations, most building activities were spontaneous. Many construction projects were illegal, and enforcement of building laws was extremely difficult. In the case of Silwan, in order to preserve the neighborhood's picturesque nature,

בנין הספריה
ע"ש ברנרד פ. ולואיס פ. בלומפילד
BERNARD M. & LOUIS M. BLOOMFIELD
LIBRARY BUILDING

the Jerusalem Municipality has developed plans based on traditional building principles and local architectural motifs.

Conservation

Whereas the idea of preserving Jerusalem's unique cityscape has always been a guiding principle, it was only during the decade since 1984 that Jerusalem's city planners began to recognize the charm and practicality of focusing upon modest urban projects. The difference this has made is truly remarkable.

Instead of complete destruction and redevelopment, preservation and revitalization of the existing urban fabric is now going hand-in-hand with heightened environmental consciousness. This is especially true

Left: Students on the campus of the Hebrew University.

Right: Young musicians
of the Conservatory of the
Jerusalem Rubin
Academy of Music and
Dance.

in the heart of downtown Jerusalem,
where the strategy changed from
comprehensive, expensive, and
monumental projects to simple and
practical solutions. Thus, the Nahlat
Shiv'a area—previously slated for
demolition—was preserved and
restored and is now one of
Jerusalem's most picturesque spots.

Among the most impressive
examples is the Mamilla neighborhood, an area of approximately
thirty acres (twelve hectares) west of
the Jaffa Gate. The original
comprehensive plan for this derelict
border area, which called for the
destruction of most existing
buildings, was scaled down and,
over a period of ten years, a more
modest and conservative plan was
implemented. Those old buildings
that were in reasonable shape were
preserved and restored and
integrated into the newly constructed areas. Today, Mamilla is a
unique urban area with residential
and commercial sections and
pedestrian malls all harmoniously
linked and resembling a small
village.

This new approach also found its
way into the suburbs, and today
modern buildings all over Jerusalem
have classic, well-defined lines and
square windows. Former extrava-
gances, such as pompous arches,
recesses, and protrusions are out.

Classics of architecture

Downtown Jerusalem has a number
of buildings which reflect
developments in modern
architecture; some are true
landmarks. Two typical—but
entirely different—examples of
architecture of the British Mandate

are the well-known King David Hotel on King David Street and the YMCA right across the street from it. The impressive King David Hotel was designed in 1930 by the Swiss architect Emil Vogt for the Egyptian-Jewish owners. With its flat, clean form and straight, rectangular lines, the symmetrical building is both beautiful and functional, and thus represents a perfect early example of the classic architectural style that has reemerged in Jerusalem over the last ten years.

The YMCA building was also built in the early 1930s. Designed by Louis Harmon, architect of the Empire State Building in New York, it is regarded as the most beautiful YMCA building in the world. The vaulted roofs and minaret-like bell tower are clearly reminiscent of Arab construction style and lend the building a distinctly Oriental character. Unlike the King David Hotel, the Jerusalem YMCA is asymmetrical, and its ornamentation makes it seem almost Baroque by comparison.

During the 1950s and 1960s, large monumental buildings became fashionable for public institutions, and in this context the Chief Rabbinate, with the adjacent Main Synagogue, came into being. Designed by architects Meir Rubin and Dr. Alexander Friedman, the buildings and their grand appearance are the target of local criticism, yet many visitors include them in their sightseeing itineraries.

Prolonged discussions concerning its architectural design preceded the Knesset building's opening in 1966. Erected on a hill opposite the Israel Museum, the striking building with its squared-off features seems to follow a neoclassical style. Three levels of administrative offices are crowned by the large assembly hall, all surrounded by square columns.

Two of Jerusalem's most impressive examples of modern architecture are the new City Hall and the Supreme Court. City Hall, regarded by its architect Jack Diamond as the high point of his career, was completed in 1993. This unique complex combines the clean functionality required by a modern administration with an aesthetically attractive style and pleasant landscaping. Its smooth white stone walls are interrupted by large windows lined with metal frames painted a light green-blue. This latter feature began to reappear in new buildings all over Jerusalem, such as the Bible Lands Museum and the Bell Mall on the corner of Jaffa Road and King George Street. According to Arab legend, the color green—or turquoise—painted around openings keeps bad spirits away from houses.

Visitors to City Hall enter from Jaffa Road through a grove of beautifully grouped tall palm trees leading onto a large square, which is lined by buildings on both sides. The square consists of three consecutive plazas, which are full of light and

Left: Israeli folk dancers.

Opposite: Micha Harari and his wife Shoshana playing harps authentically constructed to approximate David's own instruments.

provide a spacious site for ceremonies and special events.

The new Supreme Court is by far the most impressive new building in Jerusalem. Despite its instant status as an imposing monument, there is nothing inhibiting about it. In its asymmetrical layout and with its wings arranged around an inner courtyard, it is slightly reminiscent

of the Rockefeller Museum. The rows of square windows—with their original and modest ornamentation—are arranged in a manner that allows natural light into every part of the building during all hours of the day, while the building's clean-cut, linear features have an especially striking quality when illuminated at night.

Landscaping

Finally, the protection of Jerusalem's skyline and cityscape would not be complete without the landscaping which has been adopted as an integral part of urban planning. Since the first groups of Jewish immigrants returned in the late nineteenth century, the Jewish people have expressed their

Praise the Lord with harp

Rejoice in the Lord, *O ye righteous:*
  for praise is comely for the upright.
Praise the Lord *with harp:*
  sing unto him with the psaltery and an instrument of ten strings.
Sing unto him a new song; play skillfully with a loud noise.
For the word of the Lord *is right;*
  and all his works are done in truth.
He loveth righteousness and judgment:
  the earth is full of the goodness of the Lord.
By the word of the Lord *were the heavens made;*
  and all the host of them by the breath of his mouth.
He gathereth the waters of the sea together as a heap:
  he layeth up the depth in storehouses.
Let all the earth fear the Lord:
  let all the inhabitants of the world stand in awe of him.
For he spake, and it was done;
  he commanded, and it stood fast. . . .
The counsel of the Lord *standeth for ever,*
  the thoughts of his heart to all generations.

Psalm 33:1-9,11

connection with the land of Israel by planting trees. In the Jerusalem region the Jerusalem Forest along the city's southern and western borders provides a huge outdoor recreation area.

The first step towards transforming Jerusalem into a green city was the green belt, which runs around the Old City's walls and was originally designed by Sir Patrick Geddes—possibly the first modern city planner—shortly after General Allenby conquered Jerusalem in 1917. The idea was revived after 1967 by the Jerusalem Committee, so that today a lovely stretch of soft green grass protects the Old City from being suffocated by urban development.

Over the years numerous parks, public gardens, and green spaces have been created, greatly enhancing the quality of life in Jerusalem. In addition, careful attention is being paid to the preservation of Jerusalem's open spaces and scenic observation points.

The most beautiful of Jerusalem's many panoramas can be enjoyed by walking along the Haas Promenade in southern Jerusalem. Designed by the well-known architect Larry Halprin, the promenade is beautifully integrated into the hilly, desert landscape of East Talpiot and offers breathtaking views over the historic Old City of Jerusalem and beyond.

Previous spread: Part of the Ardon windows at the Jewish National and University Library (reproduced by kind permission).

Opposite: The Rebecca Crown Auditorium of the Jerusalem Music Hall.

Left: The Supreme Court Building, Jerusalem, built by the generosity of the Rothschild family.

Below: Interior of the Supreme Court Building.

Right: A modern
synagogue in the Hebrew
University area.

A living museum

Scattered throughout Jerusalem are a
number of public sculptures created
by a wide range of internationally
acclaimed artists. The idea of
Jerusalem as a living museum came
in 1968 from Arthur and Madeleine
Lejwa, who owned a well-known art
gallery in New York. In view of the
Second Commandment, "Thou shalt
not make . . . any graven image," it
seemed an unusual idea—even if
Emperor Hadrian's bust, said once to
have decorated the column at
Damascus Gate, might be considered
a first step in that direction.

But the Lejwas' idea took hold, and
public sculpture was soon accepted
by Jerusalemites. First was a work by
Hans Arp called "The Three Graces,"
placed in Jerusalem's Independence
Park next to King George Street.
Many of the other sculptures created
since have become true landmarks,
such as the "Monster"—built around
a slide at a playground in the Kiryat
Hayovel neighborhood—or
Alexander Calder's "Hommage to
Jerusalem" on Mount Herzl.

Of course, preferences are a matter
of taste, and the beholder has to
decide whether to feast the eyes on
"Jacob's Stairs"—a precast sculpture
created in 1979 by sculptor Ezra
Orionin in Miriam Garden, or on the
1993 blue-wire copy of the Statue of
Liberty by Jack Jano, placed on a
traffic island on Ben-Zvi Boulevard.

8

Jerusalem—a Modern City

"For God will save Zion, and will build the cities of Judah."
(Psalm 69:35)

Ben Yehuda Street.

Modern life in Jerusalem

Right: Street musicians in downtown Jerusalem.

The name Jerusalem usually evokes thoughts of ancient history and the three great monotheistic religions—Judaism, Christianity, and Islam. One is always keenly aware of these elements—whether walking through the city's streets, visiting one of its many museums or archaeological monuments, or enjoying a quiet moment of contemplation and prayer in one of the holy places.

But Jerusalem is also—and just as significantly—the political capital of a modern democratic state and the home of over half a million people going about their business just as in any other big city. It is a very contemporary, up-to-date city, full of life and the dynamic drive emanating from its ethnically, culturally, and professionally diverse population.

But in contrast to American cities, Jerusalem is no melting pot. Jerusalem is a kaleidoscope of national identities such as Jewish,

Below: Downtown in modern Jerusalem.

Arab, Greek, and Armenian, which have coexisted for centuries. Each group has maintained its own traditions and self-image while living and working together with the others—sometimes more successfully, sometimes less.

A city reunited
Jerusalem's reunification following the Six-Day War in 1967 was a rather sudden and unplanned-for event. For the Israelis, improvisation became a way of coping with rapidly changing developments, especially

since there were almost no precedents to go by. Teddy Kollek, mayor of Jerusalem for almost thirty years until 1993, once said, "One of the hardest lessons we had to learn was that it is easier to proclaim a state or a capital than to actually build them."[1]

The most urgent task in the reunited city was to reconstruct large parts of East Jerusalem and to bridge the gap between ancient conditions and modern requirements. The results of the tremendous efforts made over the last three decades are visible all over the city. The typical age-old cityscape was preserved and enhanced, while infrastructure and housing were developed and improved to meet the needs of a growing, twentieth-century population. To help integrate and develop Jerusalem's society and economy, new public services were established in the eastern part of town, and maintained and improved in the whole city. Traffic and communications, energy and water supply, environmental care, educational and research facilities, health services, as well as culture, sport, and recreation, and the foundations for industry and commerce—all were taken care of.

Fostering understanding

In addition, Jerusalem's reunification brought down the physical barriers

Left: A pavement violinist.

Below: Street jugglers in the shopping area.

Opposite: The softer side
of national service.

Daily life

Right: Time to relax.

of barbed wire, mine fields, and
concrete walls between two peoples
who had shared years of enmity and
war. Thus another important priority
for Jerusalem's municipality was to
encourage and foster tolerance and
understanding to ensure a peaceful
and constructive future.

Without exaggeration, most of the
achievements which make
coexistence possible in today's
Jerusalem may be attributed to the
step-by-step policies of the city's
former mayor, Teddy Kollek. In an
article which appeared in 1977 in the
American quarterly *Foreign Affairs*,
Teddy Kollek explained four
principles that helped him to ensure
the orderly continuation of everyday
life:

"1. There shall be free access to all
the Holy Places, which shall be
administered by their respective
adherents.

2. Everything possible shall be
done to ensure unhindered
development of the Arab way of life
in the Arab sections of the city, and
to ensure for the Arabs a practical
religious, cultural, and commercial
governance over their own daily
lives. The same holds true, of course,
for the various Christian communities.

3. Everything possible should be
done to ensure equal government,
municipal, and social services in all
parts of the city.

4. Continuing efforts should be
made to increase cultural, social, and
economic contacts among the
various elements of Jerusalem's
population."

In order to implement these
principles and to develop and
improve life in Jerusalem for all its
inhabitants, huge funds were needed
but were not always easy to come by.

Public and government budgets
could not hope to cover the expenses
involved. Luckily, friends of
Jerusalem found a way of creating
the means to help Jerusalem live
again, and in 1966 the Jerusalem
Foundation was founded in the
United States. This well-organized,
nonprofit body quickly grew into an
international network, raising funds
and coordinating initiatives for
valuable projects and programs for
the benefit of all residents.

It may sometimes seem a little odd

Right: Off duty.

Opposite: An Orthodox priest with his symbols of office.

to visitors to Jerusalem that so many community facilities and public buildings bear people's names. The explanation is, of course, that their construction was made possible through the generosity of the people after whom they are named.

The quality of life

From time to time there are complaints about the gap still existing between the public services available in East Jerusalem and those in the western part of town; it has already taken more than three decades to begin to make up for the neglect of centuries. And while there are many Jewish donors who generously support efforts to further improve the quality of life in the city, there are very few wealthy Arabs willing to contribute money for the common good in East Jerusalem, not least because of the pressures exerted by extremist groups.

Today all Jerusalem's inhabitants are provided with public, social, and health services. Almost every neighborhood has its own community center, offering a wide

Right: An elderly Jerusalemite.

Below: The attendant at David's Tomb, Mount Zion.

variety of cultural and recreational activities for all age groups. There are numerous libraries all over town, among which the new Arab Central Library in East Jerusalem presents a major achievement. After it opened its doors in 1992, the library quickly became a major cultural center and meeting place, especially for Arab youngsters.

In addition to the two branches of the Hadassah Hospital, there are numerous hospitals and clinics, as well as dental clinics, providing excellent health care. In this context, the Sheikh Jarrah Health Center in East Jerusalem represents an important achievement. This modern clinic is especially designed to care for the city's Arab population. Most of the doctors and nurses are Arab, a fact which makes communication and treatment easier and more comfortable for the patients. Furnished with state-of-the-art equipment, the clinic has been providing comprehensive and professional health care for the city's Arab population since 1982.

Education

Jerusalem is a city of learning and prayer. Nevertheless, its inhabitants need to earn a living, and the city has always been a place of trade. But the fact that Jerusalem had been divided for so long deterred industrial and commercial development in the city, and for many years Jerusalem was at the bottom of the ladder in per capita income in Israel.

Good schools and an extensive vocational and higher education system have proved to be indispensable for developing Jerusalem's industry and commerce. Jerusalem's youth are tomorrow's manpower—and the better skilled and equipped they are, the more able they will be to cope with the requirements of a modern, highly technological world of employment. To this end, a wide range of initiatives in the educational sector has been implemented. Old school

buildings have been renovated and equipped to meet modern requirements, new schools have been built, and vocational training programs developed. One important priority is the promotion of computer literacy—from kindergarten to high school—and an emphasis on technical subjects and skills.

Besides municipal schools, there are a great number of private schools in Jerusalem—Jewish, Christian, and Muslim—following each community's respective traditions. Special attention had to be given to the Arab population to encourage school attendance and to promote the idea of schooling for girls.

Shortly after the State of Israel was founded in 1948, compulsory school attendance was established. At that time only about twenty percent of Arab girls in the country attended school; even today, girls and boys are still instructed in separate classes. Since the early 1980s almost all Arab girls have been going to school until the age of sixteen—a fact which helps them to find jobs after graduation and become more independent.

After graduating from school, many options are open to Jerusalem's youth, including Jewish and Arab institutions of higher learning and the many vocational

Right: Nursery children of Ma'ale Adumim, a modern Jerusalem suburb.

Below: A nursery children's outing at Ma'ale Adumim.

schools. In Jerusalem, academic studies may also be pursued at the Hebrew University, founded in 1925. The university's two campuses house numerous research and development facilities and maintain many international contacts furthering academic exchange. Another attractive possibility for postgraduate studies is the Jerusalem Film and Television School, founded in 1989, which offers comprehensive training for future filmmakers and directors.

Industry

In addition to an increasing number of new shops and malls, there are

Left: A children's playground in the suburb of Ma'ale Adumim.

Opposite: A Jerusalem baker at work.

several industrial centers in the city. In the rapidly growing neighborhoods of Talpiot, Atarot, Giv'at Sha'ul, and Har Hotzvim there are a large number of factories, workshops, and medium-size businesses. To further encourage enterprise and employment, the municipality (together with the national government) founded the Jerusalem Development Authority (JDA) in 1989.

The most important economic sector being targeted by the Jerusalem Development Authority is high-tech industry. With its need for skilled personnel and its environment-friendly factories, this is well suited to Jerusalem, and in the last decade dozens of high-tech companies have opened plants in the city.

Among the large public projects that have been launched under the JDA's supervision and in cooperation with the municipality and the Israel Lands Administration is a new and comprehensive industrial and commercial center in the neighborhood of Manhat. In addition to the new high-tech industrial park being built there, housing, commerce, education, and recreation are integrated in this unique area, which is united by a "green belt" that links up with the neighboring Nahal Sorek Nature Reserve.

Among the other projects in the area—and in various stages of construction—are a spacious park around the Jerusalem Zoological Gardens, a high school of arts and sciences, a local bus terminal, and a railway station.

One of the area's most beautiful spots is the Jerusalem Mall, an impressive shopping center which offers a huge range of consumer goods. Spread over three stories, the mall houses countless new shops and department stores interspersed with snack bars, cafés, and restaurants. One can spend many hours in this bright building, whose domed glass ceilings let in the light so that the center resembles a large indoor plaza, usually buzzing with shoppers and browsers until late at night.

Another focal point for trade and exchange is the Jerusalem Convention Center, Binyanei Ha'ooma, Israel's largest facility of its kind. Numerous international academic and commercial gatherings regularly take place here, such as the Jerusalem International Book Fair, which every other year attracts hundreds of publishers and booksellers who come from all over the world to display literary works, negotiate rights, and exchange information.

I am the bread of life

And Jesus said unto them, I am the bread of life: he that cometh to me shall never hunger; and he that believeth on me shall never thirst. . . . All that the Father giveth me shall come to me; and him that cometh to me I will in no wise cast out. For I came down from heaven, not to do mine own will, but the will of him that sent me. And this is the Father's will which hath sent me, that of all which he hath given me I should lose nothing, but should raise it up again at the last day. And this is the will of him that sent me, that every one which seeth the Son, and believeth on him, may have everlasting life: and I will raise him up at the last day.

John 6:35,37-40

Traditional markets

Besides these sophisticated commercial centers, there are also Jerusalem's traditional marketplaces: Mahane Yehuda, the Jewish market, located downtown between Jaffa Road and Agrippas Street, and simply called the *shuk* by Hebrew speakers, and the picturesque Arab *suq* in the Old City. Both are colorful—and noisy—places whose fascinating appearance leaves no doubt that they belong in a Middle Eastern city. Vendors eloquently praise their goods, and one can find everything there and bargain for it— from vegetables, meat, fish, and canned foods to plastic goods, clothes, cleaning utensils, electrical appliances, cosmetics, and much more.

The time-honored custom of asking friends and relatives who are going abroad to bring back a specific brand-name article unobtainable in Jerusalem has outlived its need. Nowadays one can find everything imaginable in Jerusalem's shops, both imported products and local merchandise of high quality.

Culture

Because many different civilizations come together in Jerusalem, the city's cultural life is exceptionally rich and varied, reflecting both the diversity of the population and the desire to develop a specific Israeli cultural tradition. Each year, numerous events and festivals attract Jerusalemites as well as visitors from all over Israel and abroad—for instance, the Film Festival at the Jerusalem Cinematheque, and the Arab Film Festival, as well as the Arab Book Week. The most popular event is probably the Israel Festival held each spring, in which artists and performers from all over the world offer concerts of classical, contemporary, and folk music, theater, ballet, modern dance, and acrobatics, as well as highly original street performances throughout the city.

Jerusalem has more than forty museums, the most popular of which is the Israel Museum, founded in 1965. This is Israel's national museum and displays impressive archaeological finds, a wonderful collection of art through the ages, a design pavilion, a youth wing, a beautiful sculpture garden, and a large selection of Judaica. The neighboring Shrine of the Book houses the Dead Sea Scrolls, the famous 2000-year-old Jewish manuscripts that were found by a Bedouin shepherd boy in a cave near the Dead Sea.

Watching the world go by

One of the best places to watch Jerusalemites going about their daily business or spending their leisure time is the pedestrian mall of Ben Yehuda Street and its side streets in downtown Jerusalem. Situated within the angle formed by Jaffa

Road and King George Street, this area is one of the city's busiest shopping streets, lined with stores and pavement cafés.

On Friday mornings when most Jerusalemites start their weekends, the mall is busy with people of all ages and from all walks of life, a representative selection of city residents: elderly ladies with shopping bags, students in jeans, young parents with toddlers, an occasional soldier grabbing a quick bite at a food stand, religious men hurrying by in their black garb. Observing the action are the lucky ones able to secure one of the coffee-house chairs lining the mall. On summer nights, the area is filled with artists and craftspeople offering their work and street musicians vying for the attention of passersby.

Another picturesque pedestrian mall is Nahlat Shiv'a, a wonderful old neighborhood not far from Ben Yehuda Street. Its lovely little stone buildings house many arts and crafts shops with beautiful pottery, textiles, and jewelry, as well as attractive restaurants. Throughout the day

Below: Elevenses in Jerusalem.

Right: Tree-planting in Jerusalem.

Nahlat Shiv'a is a focal point for both Jerusalemites and visitors out to have a good time.

Eating out

Eating out is one of the special pleasures Jerusalem has to offer. Reflecting the ethnic diversity of the population, there are countless cafés, restaurants, and snack bars all over town, ranging from low-priced fast-food stalls to elegant restaurants. In East Jerusalem, as well as next to the Jewish market on Agrippas Street, innumerable small restaurants offer local Middle Eastern cuisine, while there is also a choice of Chinese, Indian, French, and Italian as well as South American, Ethiopian, and Yemeni restaurants. Modern trends have found their way into Jerusalem too, and there are now some very good vegetarian and health-food restaurants.

Jerusalemites are also fond of their cafés and coffeehouses. Whereas in East Jerusalem coffeehouses are usually sparsely decorated places frequented only by men passing their time drinking strong Turkish

Below: Pomegranates for sale.

Left: The temptation of freshly baked bread.

coffee and playing a game of sheshbesh, cafés in West Jerusalem are comfortably furnished and offer cold drinks and refreshments as well as delicious cakes and pastries.

Due to the fact that a large part of Jerusalem's population observes Jewish religious laws, many eating houses are kosher, serving either meat or dairy dishes but not both. The influence of the growing religious population and their pressure to enforce religious law in other spheres of life has led to repeated conflicts with Jerusalem's secular inhabitants.

Today a settlement has been reached in which in religious neighborhoods certain streets are closed to traffic on the Sabbath and holidays, while cultural activities and entertainment continue in other parts of the city on Friday nights and Saturdays. This is an important achievement gained by Jerusalem's municipality in order to guarantee the quality of life for all inhabitants. "The cultural institutions meet the needs of the non-religious, including last but not least, the government officials. Culture is vital to Jerusalem, if it wants to remain a modern city," as Teddy Kollek, ex-mayor of Jerusalem, explained in a recent interview.[2]

Right: A Jerusalem fruit stall.

Below: The vegetable market.

Jerusalem Versus Tel Aviv

This is also true for Jerusalem's night life. Until a decade ago, Tel Avivians used to joke about Jerusalemites and their nonexistent night life—a state of affairs which obliged them to take an hour's drive to Tel Aviv if they wanted to have some fun. But this is now no longer the case. Many pubs and bars as well as discotheques and cinemas stay open even on Friday nights, and many Jerusalemites happily take part in the city's night life.

Jerusalem's and Tel Aviv's divergent characters are perhaps partly rooted in their contrasting climates. In Tel Aviv days are hot and humid so that people come out and crowd the streets at night when it is cooler.

Even in summertime, Jerusalem nights can be chilly, and after dark a great part of the entertainment takes place indoors. Once in a while during winter, Jerusalem and the surrounding area is covered by snow for a few days. For Tel Avivians, this exotic event is a special attraction and draws from the coastal plains large numbers of spectators, who then like to take home little snowmen as mascots on the hoods of their cars.

Traffic problems and solutions
Like any big city, Jerusalem also suffers from the ailments of modern times—among them, of course, traffic problems. The older neighborhoods present a maze of narrow lanes which are difficult and sometimes impossible to negotiate with a car. Until 1982, Ben Yehuda Street presented one of the most notorious bottlenecks, causing the worst traffic jams. In addition to numerous and sometimes confusing one-way streets, the creation of traffic-reduced zones and pedestrian areas started to change things for the better.

Left: Olives for sale.

Opposite: A Jerusalem
scientific worker in the
laboratory.

Right: A Jerusalem
diamond grinder.

Modern Jerusalem's main arterial
road and its original shopping street
is Jaffa Road. Its most interesting
feature is its junction with King
George Street, where pedestrians can
also cross the street diagonally as
cars from all four directions are
stopped simultaneously. For many
years the traffic light there was the
only one in the city, and people used
to make appointments to meet at
"the" traffic light. Jaffa Road still
gets jammed during the day,
especially around the market area,
even though part of it is open for
only public transport. Although they
may disturb the harmony of the
cityscape, public parking lots have
become necessary in Jerusalem. In
addition to many privately owned
parking lots, the municipality has
gone underground with a large
parking lot under the new City Hall
and another near the Nahlat Shiv'a
pedestrian area in the center of the
city, the roof of which provides a
venue for artisans selling their work
to the public.

Israelis love to take excursions on
the weekends, and Jerusalemites are
no exception. Those who remain in
the city on Saturdays often combine
their passions for food and for the
outdoors by having a picnic or
barbecue in one of Jerusalem's many
parks and green spaces. Private
gardens are rare in Jerusalem, but
the many public gardens compensate
for this.

Right: An engineering
plant in Jerusalem.

Right: A Jerusalem fruit market.

Tourism

The Jerusalem Zoological Garden used to be confined to a relatively small area in the rather gray neighborhood of Romema. A few years ago it was relocated to a beautiful park surrounding the new urban center in southwestern Jerusalem. With its large collection of mammals, birds, and reptiles mentioned in the Bible, as well as the usual wild animals that fascinate the public, its special children's zoo with a play area, and its pony rides, it has become a major fun place for Jerusalemites of all ages.

Jerusalem's flourishing tourism is another aspect of the city's everyday life. Throughout the year hundreds of thousands of guests come from all over the world to visit Jerusalem. Jerusalem is the city with the most hotel rooms in Israel, ranging from youth hostels and simple lodgings to five-star hotels, as well as a number of kibbutz guest houses in the hills around Jerusalem. The city's central location provides the ideal starting point for trips to all parts of Israel. The many tourists from all over the world who visit Jerusalem year-round greatly add to the city's international atmosphere and are always welcome.

1. *Teddy Kollek in* My Jerusalem—Twelve Walks in the World's Holiest City, *with Shulamit Eisner, London, 1990, p. 151.*
2. *Teddy Kollek in* Focus 50, *Germany, 1993, p. 96.*

9

An Everlasting Memorial

**"As the mountains are round about Jerusalem,
so the LORD is round about his people from henceforth even for ever."**
(Psalm 125:2)

Stone sculpture by Kowatsch at Yad Vashem.

Yad Vashem

Right: The Place of Remembrance, Yad Vashem.

I n 1953 the Israeli Knesset, or parliament, passed a special law setting up Yad Vashem as a monument and memorial to the victims of the Holocaust. The Hebrew words *Yad Vashem* mean literally "an everlasting memorial," and they echo the poignant words of the prophet Isaiah: "For thus saith the LORD . . . even unto them will I give in mine house and within my walls a place and a name better than of sons and of daughters: I will give them an everlasting name, that shall not be cut off. Also the sons of the stranger, that join themselves to the LORD, to serve him, and to love the name of the LORD" (Isaiah 56:4-6).

The new law laid down that a statutory body would "gather in to the homeland material regarding all those members of the Jewish people who laid down their lives, who fought and rebelled against the Nazi enemy and his collaborators, and to perpetuate their memory and that of the communities, organizations and institutions which were destroyed because they were Jewish."

Below: A poignant sculpture at Yad Vashem.

The Holocaust

From Hitler's appointment as Chancellor of Germany in 1933, there was the impending threat of anti-Semitic activity. But at first Hitler had neither the power nor the opportunity to implement such a policy. Gradually plans were formulated. An official definition of a Jew was laid down, Jews were dismissed from their jobs, and Jewish businesses transferred to non-Jews. Vicious anti-Semitic propaganda was created by the notorious Nazi Josef Goebbels.

A watershed was *Kristallnacht* (November 9-10, 1938), when hundreds of synagogues throughout Germany were simultaneously and systematically destroyed and many

Great is thy faithfulness

I am the man that hath seen affliction by the rod of his wrath.

He hath led me, and brought me into darkness, but not into light.

Surely against me is he turned; he turneth his hand against me all the day.

My flesh and my skin hath he made old: he hath broken my bones.

He hath builded against me, and compassed me with gall and travail.

He hath set me in dark places, as they that be dead of old.

He hath hedged me about, that I cannot get out: he hath made my chain heavy.

Also when I cry and shout, he shutteth out my prayer.

He hath inclosed my ways with hewn stone; he hath made my paths crooked.

He was unto me as a bear lying in wait, and as a lion in secret places.

He hath turned aside my ways, and pulled me in pieces: he hath made me desolate. . . .

He hath filled me with bitterness, he hath made me drunken with wormwood.

He hath also broken my teeth with gravel stones, he hath covered me with ashes.

And thou hast removed my soul far off from peace: I forgat prosperity.

And I said, My strength and my hope is perished from the LORD:

Remembering mine affliction and my misery, the wormwood and the gall.

My soul hath them still in remembrance, and is humbled in me.

This I recall to my mind, therefore have I hope.

It is of the LORD'S *mercies that we are not consumed, because his compassions fail not.*

They are new every morning: great is thy faithfulness.

The LORD *is my portion, saith my soul; therefore will I hope in him.*

The LORD *is good unto them that wait for him, to the soul that seeketh him.*

It is good that a man should both hope and quietly wait for the salvation of the LORD.

It is good for a man that he bear the yoke in his youth.

Lamentations 3:1-27

Previous spread: Part of a photographic exhibit at Yad Vashem, depicting scenes from the Holocaust.

Jews killed and arrested.

Now the Nazi leaders came into the open about their aims. Hermann Goering stated: "Should the German Reich become involved in an international conflict in the foreseeable future, it goes without saying that we in Germany will have to think first and foremost about a thorough settling of accounts with the Jews within Germany." From January 1939, with the appointment of Reinhard Heydrich to achieve the "final solution," the Holocaust was under way.

By November 1943 the German Jewish population had been reduced from a total of 500,000 in 1933 to a mere 10,000. Many Jews succeeded in fleeing abroad but many others had remained, either unwilling to face the truth about the Holocaust or because there was nowhere for them to run to.

The crippled, ill, and elderly were cruelly killed in transit to the Jewish ghettos that had been set up. Those who managed to survive the impoverished, harsh, and oppressive conditions of the ghettos and the Nazis raids on them were eventually taken to the death camps.

It was not solely German Jews who were wiped out. As Germany occupied other European states, the Jews there became subject to similar isolation, ill-treatment, and eventually transportation to death camps.

Right: "Adolescence broken off."

Below: Israeli soldiers at the "Adolescence broken off" sculpture in Yad Vashem.

Yad Vashem

The monument to the Holocaust was built by the Israeli Office for the Commemoration of Martyrs and Heroes and was constructed on the Hill of Remembrance (*Har Hazi-karon*) on Mount Herzl, Jerusalem. It was completed in 1957.

Leading to the memorial is the "Avenue of the Righteous among the Nations," dedicated to non-Jews who risked and sometimes lost their lives during the Holocaust to save Jewish people. The State of Israel recognizes all these people with the honorary title "one of the righteous," and for each person so honored a carob tree may be planted with their name and nationality attached. To

date some 6000 trees have been planted here.

Perhaps best known of those represented in the Avenue of the Righteous is the Swedish diplomat Raoul Wallenberg, who started helping Jews in Hungary when he was stationed at the Swedish Embassy in Budapest. Wallenberg saved some 13,000 Jews from transportation by the Nazis, housing them in specially rented flats and announcing they were now under the protection of the Swedish government.

The Hall of Remembrance

The main memorial hall of the monument, known as the Hall of

Left: "Canyons," listing towns in Europe where Jews were killed.

Remembrance, is constructed from basalt boulders and roofed with a concrete slab. It has an unforgettable, brooding atmosphere. The floor of the vast, windowless hall is inscribed in Hebrew and Roman lettering with the names of twenty-two Nazi extermination camps—such terrible names as Chelmno, Auschwitz-Birkenau, Treblinka, Sobibor, Belzec, and Majdanek. The ashes of those killed in the camps have been brought to Israel and placed in a great vault in front of the eternal flame which burns in the hall.

Particularly moving is the separate Children's Memorial, opened in 1987. In its dark corridors are

Middle: A garden dedicated to the memory of children who died in the Holocaust.

I have cried day and night before thee

O LORD God of my salvation, I have cried day and night before thee:
Let my prayer come before thee: incline thine ear unto my cry;
For my soul is full of troubles:
    and my life draweth nigh unto the grave.
I am counted with them that go down into the pit:
    I am as a man that hath no strength:
Free among the dead, like the slain that lie in the grave,
    whom thou rememberest no more:
    and they are cut off from thy hand. . . .
Lover and friend hast thou put far from me,
    and mine acquaintance into darkness.

Psalm 88:1-5,18

recorded the names of some one-and-a-half million children who were slaughtered in the Holocaust.

The light of remembrance, an eternal flame, keeps alive forever the memory of the more than six million victims of the camps.

In adjoining rooms are found exhibits and extensive archives of the Holocaust, intended to provide a record of all those killed in the Holocaust in order to help in the continuing pursuit of perpetrators of the extermination camps and to educate future generations. The Central Archives for Holocaust Studies contain more than fifty million documents, as well as a library of some 75,000 books in many different languages.

It was evidence from the archives of Yad Vashem that helped convict the notorious Nazi war criminal Adolf Eichmann in his trial in Jerusalem in 1961 following his discovery and kidnapping in Argentina by Israeli secret service men.

The museum at Yad Vashem shows terrible photographs of the camps, mainly taken by the Nazi perpetrators, and traces the story of the Final Solution from Hitler's coming to power in 1933 until the defeat of Nazism in 1945. The Hall of Names is concerned with gathering

the names and backgrounds of those Jews killed in the Holocaust and has so far gleaned information and biographies on more than three-and-a-half million Nazi victims. The task of retrieving their names is particularly difficult, as part of the Nazi aim was to attempt to obliterate all memory of the Jews, and for this reason they destroyed many of their records. A further room, the Art Museum, displays the poignant and beautiful works of art—paintings, drawings, and sculpture—many of which were, unbelievably, created within the camps and often subsequently smuggled out.

The buildings are surrounded by a number of resonant sculptures inspired by memories of the Holocaust. The park itself is known as the Janusz Korczak Park, after the Polish teacher of that name who refused to be separated from his students and as a result was gassed in a concentration camp along with them.

One monument by Nathan Rapaport, a survivor of the Holocaust, commemorates the Warsaw ghetto uprising—a symbol of Jewish resistance to the Nazis. An identical sculpture is situated in Warsaw itself.

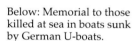

Below: Memorial to those killed at sea in boats sunk by German U-boats.

Theodor Herzl

Mount Herzl is named after the founder of Zionism, Theodor Herzl, who is buried here. Born in Budapest in 1860, Theodor Herzl was an Austrian journalist and writer. As a journalist he covered the sensational trial in Paris of the French Captain Dreyfus, a Jewish army officer who was convicted of treason to satisfy anti-Semitic sentiment in contemporary France.

Herzl was profoundly shocked by the trial and became convinced that Jews would never enjoy permanent security until they achieved a state of their own. Writing in his diary, he said: "I have the solution to the Jewish problem. Not a solution but the solution."

Herzl published his seminal book *The Jewish State* in 1896, calling for the creation of an independent Jewish state. His argument was clearly expressed; even in countries where the Jews had received equal rights they remained unassimilated and were a nation within a nation. The only answer was to establish a Jewish state; the problem was not social, economic, or religious—it was a national problem. Moreover, Herzl foresaw that anti-Semitism, as horrifyingly prefigured by the Dreyfus case, could prove disastrous for the Jews. Subsequently Herzl repeated his call for a Jewish state at the Zionist World Congress, which he summoned in Basle, Switzerland, in 1897. As a result, the formation of a national home for Jews in Palestine was adopted as policy. The Congress adopted the Basle Program: "Zionism seeks to establish a home for the Jewish people in Eretz Israel secured under public law." In his novel *Altneuland*, published in 1903, Herzl further publicized his ideas and he worked hard with political negotiations too. Theodor Herzl died in Austria in 1904.

Below: A sculpture called "The Scream of the Mother."

Above: The tomb of Theodor Herzl (1860-1904), founder of the modern State of Israel.

Right: The day of mourning for dead soldiers.

In 1949, a year after the founding of the State of Israel, Herzl was reinterred on Mount Herzl. Near his tomb a replica of his study and library have been erected as part of a museum reflecting his life and work. Several other leading Zionists and Israeli politicians, including prime ministers Golda Meir and Levi Eshkol, are buried nearby.

10

Feasts and Festivals

"The LORD is great in Zion; and he is high above all the people."
(Psalm 99:2)

A *Barmitzvah* at the Western Wall.

The Jewish Year

The Jewish calendar is marked by a number of significant festivals, most dating from Bible times.

Some are solemn, such as *Yom Kippur*, others joyful and fun, like *Purim*. All are celebrated with particular attention in the city of Jerusalem, the spiritual center of Judaism.

Right: A *Barmitzvah* at the Western Wall.

Circumcision

Jewish boys are named during the important ceremony of circumcision, which must take place on the eighth day after birth. The operation is carried out by a specially trained religious Jew known as a *mohel*, who may or may not be a rabbi or doctor. During the ceremony, the foreskin is carefully cut off. The boy is also given a Hebrew name, which is used at his *Barmitzvah*, at his wedding, and on his gravestone.

Barmitzvah

Probably the most important event in a boy's growing up is the *Barmitzvah* ceremony. (The Hebrew *Barmitzvah* means "son of the commandments.") This marks his entry into the adult community, having reached the age of thirteen. In Jewish law he is now old enough to be responsible for keeping the commandments—and for reading the *Torah* aloud in the synagogue on the Sabbath after his birthday. To be able successfully to take part in his *Barmitzvah*, a boy must be able to read Hebrew fluently so that he can

Right: Dancing at the Western Wall.

Below right: Reading Hebrew prayers at the Western Wall.

Below: Reading the Hebrew Scriptures at a *Barmitzvah*.

read from the *Torah* scroll. In preparation for the *Barmitzvah*, a Jewish boy must also know a good deal about Judaism, its rituals and beliefs.

In Jerusalem, because of the special significance of the Western Wall as a holy site, many *Barmitzvahs* take place there in the open air.

In reading from the *Torah* at his *Barmitzvah*, a number of special practices are observed by the boy. He wears a prayer shawl over his shoulders and uses the fringe of the shawl to mark his place on the scroll. He takes great care never to touch the scroll by hand because the *Torah* is regarded as sacred and must not be dirtied or damaged. The boy also wears a little black box called the *tefillin* strapped to the forehead and to the left arm, near the heart, during the ceremony. The box contains a sheet of paper containing the words known as the *Shema*: "Hear O Israel, the Lord our God is one God. You shall love the Lord your God with all your heart, soul and strength." The *tefillin* are tied on in response to the biblical injunction in Deuteronomy 6:6-8 to keep the words on their foreheads and on their hearts.

The *Barmitzvah* is a time of great rejoicing, and there is usually a

special party for family and friends when the boy will also be expected to make a speech as a young man. He will receive many presents, foremost among which will probably be religious objects such as *tefillin;* the *tallit*, or prayer shawl; and the *kippah*, the prayer cap which is always to be worn to keep the head covered in reverence to God.

Marriage

The Jewish people hold marriage in very high esteem. The wedding itself does not have to take place in a synagogue, though most do. However, the bride and groom must stand beneath a special canopy, or *huppah*, which is often beautifully decorated with flowers. The canopy, usually supported on four poles, symbolizes their new marital home. The bride and groom are given wine to drink and vow to practice the Jewish religion together. The groom gives his bride a ring and makes a

special vow in Hebrew. After he has signed the marriage certificate (*ketubah*), which pledges him to his wife, the bridegroom crushes a glass under his foot. No one quite knows what the significance of this action is; some suggest it is done in memory of the destruction of the Temple by the Romans in 70 A.D.; others say that it symbolizes the idea that even a festival of great joy must not pass without a reminder that there are also more serious times—and that they should remember those who are less happy than they are.

Sabbath (*Shabbat*)

Sabbath is observed every week. Sabbath begins just before sunset on Friday evening and finishes after sunset on Saturday. Sabbath commemorates the creation of the world, when God is said to have rested on the seventh day, and also commemorates the deliverance of the Hebrews from slavery in Egypt.

The Fourth Commandment says: "Remember the Sabbath day and keep it holy. Six days you shall work, and the seventh day is the Sabbath of the Lord your God. . . . For in six days the Lord made heaven, the earth, the sea and all that is in them; therefore the Lord blessed the seventh day and made it holy."

In Orthodox homes, any work—even switching on the gas or electricity—is forbidden on the Sabbath, so a great deal of preparation has to be done on Friday. Cooking and cleaning must all be completed before sundown.

Shabbat starts with the woman of the house lighting at least two candles. The *Shabbat* greeting is, *"Shabbat Shalom"*—"a peaceful Sabbath to you." The men or sometimes the entire family go to synagogue. But the focus of the evening is the special meal with all the family present, which starts with the blessing and drinking of wine

Opposite: Women in their designated area at the Western Wall greet a young man at his *Barmitzvah*.

Right: A grandfather helps his grandson at his Western Wall *Barmitzvah*.

and the blessing of the day, a ceremony known as *kiddush*. The prayer opens, "Blessed art thou, O Lord our God, King of the Universe who creates the fruit of the vine. . . ."

The meal itself then begins with the blessing of the bread, consisting of two special twisted or braided loaves, *challah*. These represent the double portion of manna which was collected on the day before the Sabbath at the time when the Israelites were wandering in the wilderness. Special *Shabbat* songs are sometimes sung during the meal. Often the family will entertain guests; Jewish people feel it would be wrong for any Jew to eat his or her Sabbath meal alone.

On *Shabbat* morning often the entire family will go to the synagogue. The remainder of the day is a day of rest, when ordinary duties and tasks are put aside. The family might go for a walk, play games, visit friends, or study the *Torah*.

Sabbath finishes with another little ceremony called *Havdallah*, meaning "separation." The father praises God, who separated darkness from light, the Sabbath from the rest of the week, and Abraham from the other nations. All this he symbolizes by holding a lighted taper which he shields with his hands. A special plaited candle is lit. A box of sweet spices symbolizes the fragrance of the Sabbath day, which should be carried over into the coming week. As wine is poured over a candle, the family wish one another a good week.

Make a joyful noise unto God

Make a joyful noise unto God, all ye lands:
Sing forth the honor of his name:
    make his praise glorious.
Say unto God, How terrible art thou in thy
    works! Through the greatness of thy power
    shall thine enemies submit themselves unto
    thee.
All the earth shall worship thee, and shall sing
    unto thee;
    they shall sing to thy name. Selah.
Come and see the works of God: he is terrible
    in his doing toward the children of men.
He turned the sea into dry land:
    they went through the flood on foot:
    there did we rejoice in him . . . .
O bless our God, ye people, and make the
    voice of his praise to be heard.

Psalm 66:1-6,8

Previous spread: People
pray at the Western Wall
at *Yom Kippur*.

Right: A wedding takes
place inside a special
"tent" erected within a
room.

Right: A circumcision
takes place in Jerusalem.

Rosh Hashanah

Jewish New Year, known as *Rosh Hashanah*, meaning "Head of the Year," comes in September or October. It is the first day of the civil year—but, confusingly, the seventh month of the religious year. It is celebrated in the home with joy; but it is also a solemn occasion. It marks the commemoration of the creation of the world, but also judgment. The Jewish Prayer Book explains: "This is the day that the world was called into existence. This day he caused all creatures to stand in judgment."

After *Rosh Hashanah* there follow ten days of penitence, when it is believed that God will assess the good and evil each person has committed. Jewish tradition has it that on New Year's Day God sits in judgment; before him are three great books. The first contains the names of the good; the second the names of the bad; and the third the names of those who are neither very good nor very bad! While he gives judgment

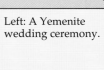

Left: A Yemenite
wedding ceremony.

Passover

And ye shall observe the feast of unleavened bread; for in this selfsame day have I brought your armies out of the land of Egypt: therefore shall ye observe this day in your generations by an ordinance for ever.

Exodus 12:17

Right: A Jewish family unites to celebrate *Seder*, the commemoration of the Passover.

immediately on those whose names are found in the first two books, those in the third are given ten days—till *Yom Kippur*—to attempt by prayers, repentance, and good deeds to have their names moved to the first book. So these ten days assume great importance for Jews, who of course want to do all they can to ensure that their names appear in the first book.

On the eve of *Rosh Hashanah* just before the evening meal, everyone dips pieces of apple in honey and eats them; this symbolizes the hope that the coming year will be prosperous and sweet.

At the Western Wall and in synagogues throughout Judaism, the ram's horn (known as the *shofar*) is blown on this day. It reminds the people of the ram sacrificed in Isaac's place by Abraham, and it is also in obedience to the scriptural command: "And the Lord said to Moses, 'Say to the people of Israel, "In the seventh month, on the first day of the month, you shall observe a day of solemn rest, a memorial proclaimed with blast of trumpets. a holy convocation."'" (The feast is sometimes also known as the Feast of Trumpets.) The blowing of the horn also serves to remind people that the Day of Atonement is approaching so that they can prepare for it.

Yom Kippur

Ten days after *Rosh Hashanah* comes *Yom Kippur*, the Day of Atonement. This is the holiest and most solemn day in the Jewish year, as it is when it is believed God makes his judgment, forgiving those who have truly repented. "On the tenth day of this seventh month there shall be a day of atonement: it shall be a holy convocation unto you; and ye shall afflict your souls. . . . And ye shall do no work in that same day: for it is a day of atonement, to make an atonement for you before the Lord your God" (Leviticus 23:27,28).

In the time of the Temple, this was the one day in the year when the

high priest sacrificed for the sins of the people of Israel and entered the holiest place.

So it is important for observant Jews that the previous days have been spent in prayer. On *Yom Kippur* itself, the more devout Jews spend the entire day in the synagogue and neither eat nor drink from sunset on the previous evening until after sundown the next day. Some beat their breast as a sign of contrition.

Succoth

Not long after *Yom Kippur* comes the Feast of Tabernacles. By contrast with the Day of Atonement, it is a

very happy time. This is the third of the Great Feasts and is mentioned frequently in the Bible. It is a feast of great rejoicing, as it is in effect harvest thanksgiving (there are three harvest festivals in the Jewish year, the others occurring at Passover and Pentecost), and also a time of remembering with thanks God's protection of the Israelites during their forty years' journeying through the wilderness.

The word *Succoth* means "booth," and many families build a booth or *Succoth* on the roof or in the garden. The booth is a little hut or shelter decorated with fruit and leaves; and

God is our refuge and strength

God is our refuge and strength, a very present help in trouble.
Therefore will not we fear, though the earth be removed, and though the
mountains be carried into the midst of the sea. . . .
There is a river, the streams whereof shall make glad the city of God, the
holy place of the tabernacles of the Most High.

Psalm 46:1,2,4

Previous spread: A text in fire marks the climax of a military oath-taking ceremony for new army recruits.

Celebration

families often eat their meals in it during the festival—even sleeping there too if the climate permits (the shelter has no roof). The booth reminds the Jewish family of how God protected them when they had no permanent homes during their travels through the wilderness following the exodus from Egypt.

During synagogue services, people wave willow leaves, myrtle, palm branches, and the citrus fruit etrog in every direction to show that God is to be found everywhere and in all countries.

Simchat Torah
The final day of *Succoth* is called *Simchat Torah*, which means "rejoicing in the *Torah*," or Law. It marks the end of the annual cycle of readings from the *Torah*. All the *Torah* scrolls are taken out of the Ark where they are normally stored and processed round the synagogue. The people carrying the scrolls often

dance with them in celebration and the children join in, waving flags. The final words of Deuteronomy (the last book of the Law) and the first words of Genesis (the first book of the Law) are read out loud to show that God's word never ends.

Hanukkah
This feast is often also known as the Festival of Lights and falls in December, quite near to the Christian festival of Christmas. It celebrates the rededication of the Second Temple in the time of the

Below: Dressing up for *Purim.*

Bottom: Children celebrate *Purim.*

Left: Masked and costumed for *Purim* celebrations.

Maccabees in 165 B.C. The armies of Antiochus Epiphanes of Syria had captured Jerusalem in 175 B.C., and ritually defiled the Temple by taking idols into the holy place and by sacrificing a sow. When the Jews, led by the heroic Judas Maccabeus, finally expelled the invading army and regained the Temple, they instituted the Feast of Dedication, or Lights, to commemorate this victory.

For this feast a special nine-branched candlestick is used to commemorate the miracle of the oil. This story, retold in the extra-canonical Book of Maccabees, tells how the priests, after cleaning and purifying the holy place, discovered

Below: Celebrations for the festival of *Simchat Torah.*

Lights and lots

there was only one small vessel of oil with which to fill the seven-branched candlestick inside the holy place. Oil for the lamps took eight days to prepare correctly, so the priests had to decide whether to light the lamps immediately or await new supplies. They decided on the first option, lighting the lamp from the little vessel. Miraculously, the lights continued burning for the full eight days until the new supply of oil was ready.

For this reason the Feast of Lights lasts eight days. Each day candles are lit in the *menorah*, the special candlestick with nine branches. (The ninth candle is the "servant," used to light the others.) During this festival, children often play a special game with a top called a *dreidle*.

Pesach

The most well-known Jewish festival is Passover, or in Hebrew, *Pesach*. Along with Pentecost and Tabernacles, this is known as one of the Great Feasts, as it was commanded in the Law of Moses, the Pentateuch. It falls at roughly the same time as the Christian Easter, and celebrates the escape of the Hebrews from the land of Egypt—and in particular the night when the Angel of Death

> ## The feast of tabernacles
> *And the* LORD *spake unto Moses, saying, Speak unto the children of Israel, saying, The fifteenth day of this seventh month shall be the feast of tabernacles for seven days unto the* LORD*.... And ye shall take you on the first day the boughs of goodly trees, branches of palm trees, and the boughs of thick trees, and willows of the brook; and ye shall rejoice before the* LORD *your God seven days.*
>
> Leviticus 23:33,34,40

"passed over" the Hebrews' houses, visiting only the Egyptian homes.

The Hebrews left Egypt so quickly that they had no time to let their bread rise before they left, so they were instructed to make flat bread without yeast. For this reason, at Pesach Jewish families eat unleavened flat bread, known in Hebrew as Matzos to remind them of

the very first Passover.

Before the feast the house has to be cleaned completely; any food containing yeast must be thrown away, because this is the feast of the unleavened bread. Unleavened bread is also a reminder of the bread of affliction, which the Hebrew people ate during their slavery in Egypt.

Previous spread: (left) A young man reads the Hebrew Scriptures at the Western Wall; (right) Blowing the *shofar* horn at the Western Wall for the festival of *Rosh Hashanah*.

Above: The Fire Festival.

Opposite: The Fire Festival.

Seder

On the first two nights of the festival of *Pesach* the family gathers to celebrate the *Seder*, during which they read from the *Haggadah*, the story of God's deliverance of the Hebrews from Egyptian slavery. (*Haggadah* means "telling the story.") The youngest child asks: "Why is this night so different from all other nights?"—and the *Haggadah* answers that question.

On the table are assembled all the special *Seder* foods, each with its special significance. Each item recalls the story of the exodus, found in the Book of Exodus chapters 1-12. A hard-boiled egg is a reminder of the birth of the nation of Israel; a roasted lamb's bone represents the Passover lamb once sacrificed in the Temple (the Jews believe that sacrifice can only be made in Jerusalem at the appointed place; today no sacrifices are made); bitter herbs remind the Jewish family of the bitter lives their forefathers endured as slaves in Egypt; fresh vegetables such as cucumber remind them that this is a springtime feast; the *Haroseth*, a mixture of chopped apple, nuts, cinnamon, and wine remind them of the mud that the Hebrew slaves used to make bricks for the Egyptians— and also of the sweetness of freedom; saltwater represents the tears of the Hebrew captives; a sprig of parsley

Blow the trumpet!

Sing aloud unto God our strength:
  make a joyful noise unto the God of Jacob.
Take a psalm, and bring hither the timbrel,
  the pleasant harp with the psaltery.
Blow up the trumpet in the new moon
  in the time appointed, on our solemn feast day.
For this was a statute for Israel,
  and a law of the God of Jacob.

Psalm 81:1-4

Right: The Western Wall
at the Feast of
Tabernacles.

Below right: A woman
prays at the Western
Wall.

Thou, LORD, knowest

O LORD, thou hast searched me,
    and known me.
Thou knowest my downsitting
    and mine uprising; thou understandest
    my thought afar off.
Thou compassest my path and my lying
    down, and art acquainted with all my
    ways.
For there is not a word in my tongue,
    but, lo, O LORD, thou knowest it altogether.
Thou hast beset me behind and before,
    and laid thine hand upon me.
Such knowledge is too wonderful for me;
    it is high, I cannot attain unto it.
Whither shall I go from thy spirit?
    or whither shall I flee from thy presence?
If I ascend up into heaven, thou art there:
    If I make my bed in hell, behold, thou art
    there.
If I take the wings of the morning,
    and dwell in the uttermost parts of the sea;
Even there shall thy hand lead me,
    and thy right hand shall hold me.

Psalm 139:1-10

Left: At the Western Wall
with the *Torah*.

shoot bows and arrows to emulate Bar Kochba.

Left: A father and young son at the Western Wall.

Pentecost (*Shavuot*)

The word *Pentecost* is derived from the Greek word for "fiftieth"; *Shavuot* is the Hebrew word for "weeks." *Shavuot* marks the giving of the Ten Commandments on Mount Sinai and also harvest, and is the third Great Feast. It comes on the fiftieth day after Passover and is described in Exodus 23:16 as "the feast of harvest, the first fruits of thy labors, which thou hast sown in the field." Although it began as an agricultural feast, a sort of harvest festival, *Shavuot* is now marked more as the Giving of the Law. It was on the fiftieth day after the first Passover that Moses ascended Mount Sinai to receive the Ten Commandments. The harvest significance is not forgotten; the synagogue is usually decorated with plants and flowers, and this is a time when dairy produce is eaten.

During the synagogue services the Ten Commandments are read, and some Jewish people sit upright through the night contemplating God's Law.

Passover is followed by a period of seven weeks' mourning. This remembers the failure of the Jewish revolt against the Romans in 70 A.D. and the deaths of a number of Jewish teachers and scholars at about the same time.

Day of Mourning

On the ninth day of the Jewish month Av (*Tishah B'Av*) the Jews remember the destruction of Herod's Temple in 70 A.D. and also the destruction of the first Temple by

stands for the hyssop bunch with which the blood of the Passover lamb was splashed on the lintel and doorposts on the first Passover; and two lighted candles symbolize God's guiding hand as he led the Hebrews out of Egypt.

By eating these dishes and drinking wine, the Jews remind themselves of the escape from slavery to freedom. Four cups of wine are drunk: the Cups of Sanctification, Redemption, Blessing, and Thanksgiving. The family also leaves an empty place for the prophet Elijah, with a glass of wine ready for him; it is believed that his return will herald the coming of the Messiah.

Lag B'Omer

The period between *Pesach* and *Shavuot* is very solemn. The Jews remember their suffering at the hands of the Romans. These are the days of counting (*sefira*).

The only exception to this solemnity is the festival of *Lag B'Omer*, which is celebrated with bonfires and picnics. On this day Orthodox Jews build a fire and dance around the grave of the rabbi Simeon ben Yochai to remember the day he revealed the secrets of Jewish mysticism to his followers. Other ancient heroes are also commemorated—the warmly remembered Rabbi Akiba, and the leader of the Jewish rising, Bar Kochba. Children

Opposite: Face-painting
at *Purim*.

Purim

Right: Something to
celebrate.

Nebuchadnezzar in 586 B.C. Many
Jewish people fast for twenty-four
hours. In the synagogue the men sit
on the floor or on very low stools.
The curtain of the Ark (containing
the *Torah*) is removed and the lights
are dimmed; all this symbolizes the
destruction of the Temple. It is the
saddest day in the year.

Purim

The origins of the festival of *Purim*
are found in the Book of Esther,
where we discover how Queen
Esther saved her people from the
plans of the wicked Haman when
the Jews were in exile in Persia
during the reign of King Ahasuerus.
Haman was plotting to massacre the
entire Jewish people, but the Jewish
queen Esther intervened with the
king, successfully saving her people.
The word *Purim* derives from the
Hebrew word for "lots," and refers
to the lots cast by Haman to decide
which was the best day on which to
carry out his planned massacre.

In the synagogue the story of
Esther is read aloud at *Purim* from a
specially decorated scroll; each time
Haman is mentioned, the children
make the loudest noise they can—
hissing, stamping, rattling, and
banging. Sometimes they even write

the name "Haman" on the soles of
their shoes, so that his name is
"blotted out" as the children stamp
their feet.

After the service there are *Purim*
cakes to eat. Often children—and
adults too—dress up, and there are
also traditional plays called
purimspiel. In Israel this becomes a
sort of carnival time with street
parades and lots of fancy dress.
There are also special cakes known
as *Hamantaschen*.

Right: A procession at the
Feast of Tabernacles.

Two Orthodox Jews on
the empty streets of
Jerusalem on *Yom Kippur*.

INDEX

*Figures set in italic denote
photographs*

Abraham 66
Aceldama *166-167*
Alexander the Great 48
Allenby, Edmund 53, 65
Altar of the Crucifixion 86
Ain Karim *147*
Alexander III 154
Anglican churches
    Christ Church 109
    St George's Cathedral 109
Antiochus III 48
Antiochus IV (Epiphanes) 48, 49,
    70
Araunah 66
archaeology *14*
Ardon windows *171, 190-191*
Aristobulus 49
Armenian Cathedral of St James
    101, 103, 107-108
Armenian Quarter *100*
Armenians 104, 108
Artaxerxes 46
arts *171-194*
Ashkenazi Jews 123, 130
Assyrian Empire 38
Atonement, Day of *see Yom Kippur*

Babylon 40, 44, 46
Baldwin 51
Balfour Declaration 53
Barmitzvah 124-125, 223, 224-229
bazaar *67*
Ben Yehuda Street *195*
Bethany *52-53*
Beth-El 38
Bethesda 82, *83*, 88, 90
Bethphage 156
Bezalel School of Art *172*
Bloomfield Park *164-165*
British Mandate 53
Broad Wall *134*
Bucharan Quarter 176
building materials 172-173, 176
Burnt House 126, *135*

Caiaphas' house 156, 162
Calvary 87; *see also* Golgotha
cardo maximus 130, 135
cemeteries *59*
Chapel of Sorrows 86
Chapel of the Exaltation of the
Cross 86
Chapel of the Holy Sepulchre 86
churches
    All Nations 97, 100, *152*
    Ascension 100

Christ Church 109
Disciples and Ascension 100
Dominus Flevit 100
Dormition *29, 58-59*, 109, *159*
Holy Sepulchre *13*, 50, *78-86,
    90-93, 96-97, 104, 105*
Holy Trinity 103, *170*
Nea 109
Pater Noster 100
Redeemer *102, 103*, 108-109
St Anne 86, 88
St George 109
St James *101*, 103, 107-108
St Mark 100, *103, 108*
St Mary Magdalene *37*, 94
St Peter in Gallicantu 162
circumcision 225, *232*
Citadel *38-43*, 160
City Hall 187
City of David Archaeological
    Garden *14*
clothing 139-140
Coenaculum 150-151, 156, 158
conservation 185-186
Constantine 50
convents
    St Onuphrius 167
Crusaders 50-52, 81
Crypt of St Helena 86
Cyrus 10, 46

Damascus gate 7
Darius 46
Day of Atonement *see Yom Kippur*
Dead Sea Scrolls *175-177*
Dedication, Feast of *see Hannukah*
Development Authority 204
David 10, 32-33, 66
Dome of the Chain *75*
Dome of the Rock 10, 12, *13, 37*, 62,
    65, 66, *72-77*

East Jerusalem 184-185
Ecce Homo arch *78*
education *202-203*; *see also* schools;
    Hebrew University; Rubin
    Academy
Egypt 32, 40, 48
Esther 250
Et-Tur 100, 156
Exile
    in Assyria 38
    in Babylon 44, 46
    in Egypt 32
Exodus 32
Ezion-Geber 36
Ezra 48

festivals *223-252*; *see also* individual
    festivals
Fire Festival *see Lag B'Omer*
    forestry 193
Franciscan Dominus Flevit Chapel
    100
Frederick Barbarossa 52

Gabbatha 157, 160
Garden Tomb *162-163*, 166
gates 137-146
    Damascus *7*, 62, *168*
    Golden *36*, 64
    Jaffa *44, 45*, 65
    Mandelbaum 60
    St Stephen's *44*, 62, *169*
Gethsemane *37*, 94, *152-155*, 158,
    160
Gihon Spring 26, 30, 33, 36
Godfrey de Bouillon 50
Golgotha 80, 81, *161*, 166
Gordon, Charles 160, 166
Goren, Shlomo *20-21*
Gregorian Church 107

Hadrian 49
Haggadah 246
Hannukah 49, 238-239, 242
Haram Al Sharif 62, 74, 76-77
Harel, Du-Du *172-173*
harp *189*
Hasidic Jews 123, 138
health service 202
Hebrew University *184-185*, 203
Hellenism 48
Herod the Great 10, 49, 70-72, 161
Herzl, Theodor 221-222
Hezekiah's Tunnel *15, 33*
Hiram of Tyre 70
Holocaust 214
House of Caiaphas 156
housing 176-177
Hyrcanus 49

Ibrahim Pasha 130
industry 203-204
Israel 38, 53, 54
Israelite Tower 125-126
Issos 48

James, son of Zebedee 107
Jebusites 33
Jehoiachin 44
Jehoiakim 40, 44
Jeroboam 38
Jerusalem Committee 182
Jesus of Nazareth 49, 148-169
Jewish Quarter *18*, 123, *134*, 173
Josiah 38
Judah 38, 49
Judas Iscariot 167
Judas Maccabeus 49
Justinian 109

Kennedy Memorial 183
Kidron Valley *35, 50-51*
King David Hotel 187
Kiryat Hayovel 177
Knesset *54-55, 60*, 187
Kollek, Teddy 60

Lag B'Omer 246, 247, 249
Last Supper 156
    Hall of the *150-151, 156, 158*

League of Nations 53
libraries 202; *see also*
 Ardon windows
 Gulbenkian 108
 Hebrew University *184-185*
 Yad Vashem *215*
Lights *see Hannukah*
limestone 172-173
Lutheran Church of the Redeemer *102, 103,* 108-109

Maccabean wars 49, 71
Mameluks 52
Mamilla 186
manuscripts *23, 108*
maps *9-11*
markets *70-71, 204, 208, 212*
marriage 226; *see also* weddings
Mattathiah 49
Mea Shearim 138, 176
menorah 24, 144, 242
Mishkenot Sha'anim 175-176
Moab *25*
Montefiore windmill *47*
mosques
 El Aqsa 50, *60, 62, 65,* 74, *76-77, 81*
Mount Moriah *66*
Mount of Olives *8, 31, 59, 60, 149*
Mount Zion 150-151, *200*
mourning *see Tishah B'Av*
Muhammad 50, 74
museums *see also*
 Shrine of the Book; Yad Vashem
 Ben Swil *174*
 Israel 17, *178, 204*
 Herzl 222
 History of Jerusalem *38*
 Modern Art *182*
 Rockefeller *175*
music *186, 189, 196, 197*
Music Hall *180-181, 193*
Muslims 50, 52

Nahlat Shiva 176, 186, 206-207
Nebuchadnezzar 10, 40, 44
neighborhoods 175-178, 182-186
New Jerusalem 167-170
New Year *see Rosh Hashanah*

olive trees *153*
Ottoman Empire 52

parks *8*
Passover *see Pesach*
Pavement *see Gabbatha*
Pentecost *see Shavuot*
Persia 46, 48
Pesach 242, 249; *see also Seder*
Philippe Auguste 52
planning 172-173, 176, 182, 184-186
Pompey 49
Praetorium *39, 160*
Ptolemy 48
Purim 238, 239, 250

Ramot Allon 183
Rehavia neighborhood 176
Rehoboam 38
Robinson's Arch *117,* 120
Rosh Hashanah 232, 234, *245*
Rubin Academy of Music and Dance *186*
Russian Orthodox Cathedral of the Holy Trinity 103, *117*
Russian Orthodox Church of St Mary Magdalen at Gethsemane 37, 154-155

Sabbath *see Shabbat*
Saladin 52
Saul 32
schools *139; see also Yeshiva*
scrolls *23, 128, 137, 139, 145; see also*
 Dead Sea Scrolls
Seder 234-235
Seleucids 48
Sephardic Jews 123
Shabbat 226-228
Shavuot 249
Shishak 70
shofar 115, 120, 245
shops *66, 69*
Shrine of the Book *176-177*
Siloam *57*
Silwan 184-185
Simchat Torah 238-239
Simon bar Kochba 49
Six-Day War 60
Solomon 10, 34, 36, 66
Solomon's Pools *56*
Solomon's Quarries 62
Stations of the Cross
 see Via Dolorosa
suburban neighborhoods 175-178, 182-186
Succoth 234, 238, 240-243, 248, 250, 251
Suleiman the Magnificent 52, 62
Supreme Court 188, *193*
synagogues 130, *141, 194*
 Renanim *142-145*
 Great *146*
 Hurvah *13, 24,* 130-131
 Ramban 130
 Sephardic *130,* 132
 Tiferet Israel 131
Syrian Orthodox Church of St Mark 100, *103, 108*

Tabernacles *see Succoth*
Talpiot 184
Tel Aviv 208
Temple 10, 34, 36, 44, 49, 66, 70-73, 76, 79, 112-114, *142*
Temple Mount *32-33,* 65, *74-81*
tephillim 122, 124-125
Tishah B'Av 249-250
Titus 49
tombs of
 Absalom *35*
 Bene Hezir *34*

David *128, 132-133,* 134, *200*
Theodor Herzl 222
Herod family *164-165*
Jesus *162-163*
Lazarus *52*
Sanhedrin or Judges *16-17*
Torah scrolls *23, 128, 137, 145*
tourism *212*
Tower of David *42*
traffic 209-210
Turks 52

university *see Hebrew University*
Upper Room 156
Urban II 50

Via Dolorosa 78, *86-89,* 173

Wailing Wall *see Western Wall*
walls 49; *see also* Broad Wall; gates; Western Wall
War of Independence 12, 55
water *56-57*
weddings *232, 233; see also* marriage
Western Wall *18, 20-21, 22,* 72, *111-136,* 223, 224-231, *244-245, 248, 249*
 tunnels 76, *78*
Wilhelm II 65
Wilson's Arch 120
windmills *47*

Yad Vashem *214-222*
Yemin Moshe 176
Yeshiva 132, *138, 139*
Yiddish 140
YMCA 187
Yom Kippur 115, *230-231,* 234, *252*

Zechariah, Tomb of *34*
Zedekiah 44
Zerubbabel 70
Zoological Garden 212

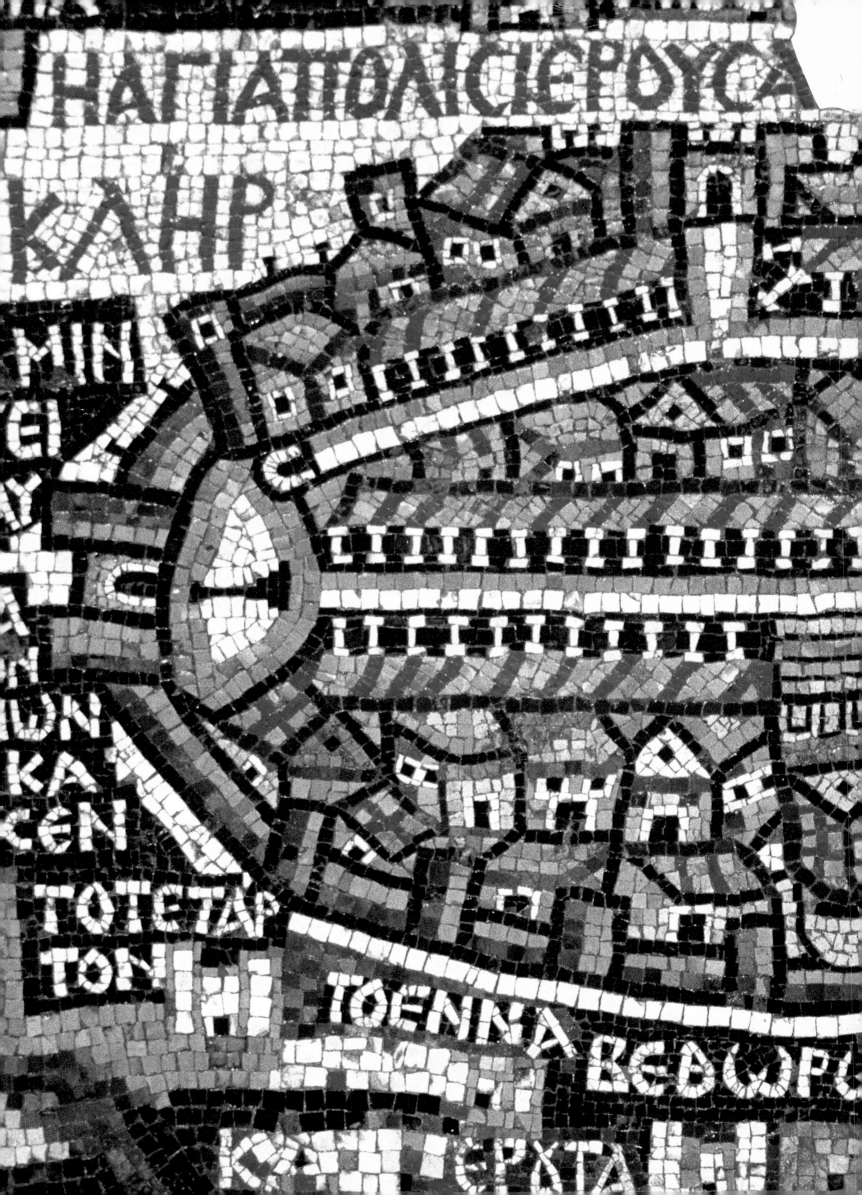